ADVANCED BUSH CRAFT

An Expert Field Guide — to the Art of — WILDERNESS SURVIVAL

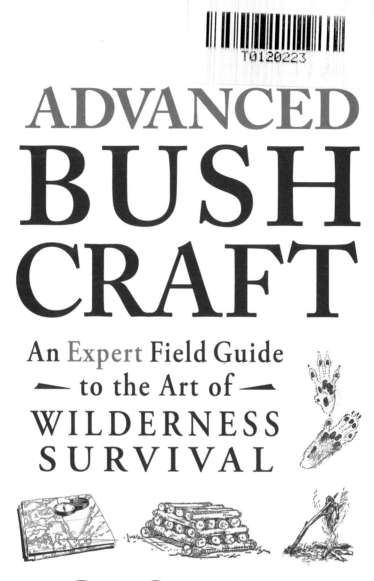

DAVE CANTERBURY
New York Times Bestselling Author of *Bushcraft 101*

Adams Media
New York   London   Toronto   Sydney   New Delhi

Adams Media
An Imprint of Simon & Schuster, Inc.
100 Technology Center Drive
Stoughton, MA 02072

For information about special discounts for bulk purchases, please contact Simon & Schuster Special Sales at 1-866-506-1949 or business@simonandschuster.com.

The Simon & Schuster Speakers Bureau can bring authors to your live event. For more information or to book an event contact the Simon & Schuster Speakers Bureau at 1-866-248-3049 or visit our website at www.simonspeakers.com.

Interior illustrations by Eric Andrews copyright © Simon & Schuster, Inc.
The line drawing on page 46 was rendered from a photograph copyright © 2011 by Mark Emery and used with permission.

Manufactured in the United States of America

22 2023

Library of Congress Cataloging-in-Publication Data has been applied for.

ISBN 978-1-4405-8796-2
ISBN 978-1-4405-8797-9 (ebook)

DEDICATION

A book should be dedicated not only to those from whom the knowledge to write it was secured but also for those who make it possible. My wife Iris has made it possible for me to live my dream of teaching outdoor skills to others through many outlets from social media to television as well as the written word. She has faithfully stood by me through the countless hours of training and evolving, through the years of practice and experimental dirt time. She has always supported me and given of herself to help fulfill my dreams in this and any endeavor, and so to her I dedicate this book. I would also like to thank my father for the examples in work ethic he taught me my entire life and still to this day. While we strive to chase our dreams in life we must always remember the road to success is paved by the work you put into it. I have learned this lesson well from his teachings.

As for the contents of this book, the list is exhaustive to say the least: men forgotten in history of both American and European descent, native peoples of the early Americas who passed their knowledge to us along the way in the early days of exploration, and many modern role models who continue to this day to pass on the knowledge they have in an effort to establish these lessons for generations to come. The writings of authors past such as Daniel Beard, Ernest Thompson Seton, Hyatt Verrill, William Hamilton Gibson, George Washington Sears, Horace Kephart, Mors Kochanski, and many others come to mind quickly as shining examples of men from whom I have taken a wealth of knowledge to further my learning.

ACKNOWLEDGMENTS

At the end of the day we must realize where the knowledge we have gained even comes from to begin with. For me this is a complicated question indeed. As I began this journey, I was not at all accomplished in the aspects of social media, didn't even know what YouTube was, and—as I have learned—there was not much information about bushcraft in that media stream. So, for me, the learning came from two sources: research and practical exercise.

Reading has always been my favorite form of research, and there are mountains of books on every facet of the skills needed for self-reliance if you are willing to search them out. Authors such as Hyatt Verrill, Warren Hastings Miller, Francis Buzzacott, and, of course, George Washington Sears and Horace Kephart have published much on this topic. In the modern day we have many authors who can help us gain knowledge in this area as well, and some of them, like Bradford Angier and Mors Kochanski, are now considered standards. We have access to the Internet, which has opened many doors that were never available thirty years ago. To such great thinkers as Vint Cerf, who enabled us to pass information across the boundaries of the seas in instant fashion, we owe a great deal.

CONTENTS

— Introduction —

This is the second in what I hope will eventually be a series of books on the art of bushcraft, or wilderness survival. *Bushcraft 101* was a primer on the skills necessary for a short stay in the wilderness. These skills include building an effective kit, selecting and managing equipment, developing supplies, and setting up camp. Much of our study was on connecting with nature and learning the basics for preparing ourselves for any climate and situation. In *Bushcraft 101* we learned that many things can be accomplished with our own knowledge and a few tools. We talked about the kinds of things you need for a short stay outdoors. In *Advanced Bushcraft*, we will take these skills to the next level and prepare you for a lengthy stay in the wilderness.

The most important thing to understand before embarking on a long journey outdoors is resource management. You can only carry so much on your back—especially if you plan to hike or walk for a long distance. Since you cannot bring a truckload of supplies with you, you need to understand the limitations of your kit and how to maximize the environment and its resources to overcome these limitations. You must discern between which supplies you should carry with you and which can be harvested or manufactured on the trail. This requires keen competency in manufacturing versatile tools, starting fires with minimal forms of ignition, developing semipermanent shelter, and establishing an effective trapping campaign for food.

Long-term sustainability will require a lot of improvisation. Part of self-reliance is learning to deal with the unexpected. Tools will break, weather will turn, and food sources may be hard to find. You need to be confident enough in your skills that you can fix the handle on your axe if it breaks, and, when you do find that game, preserve the leftovers so the meat will last you a good while. If you understand advanced skills such as building watercraft and making containers for water and other supplies, you will be able to negotiate the climate and your environment for a long time. Don't underestimate the value of comfort. If you are going to be out for a long time, a good night's sleep is critical. Knowing how to assemble a sleep system by fashioning pillows and building raised beds will make a tremendous difference in your ability to be successful.

We will also take a close look at advanced wilderness skills such as weaving for additional clothing and shelter implements and net making to help secure fish and other water animals as additional sources of protein. Managing cordage and manufacturing additional rope out of natural materials will be a critical component of these practices.

Understanding the natural world will be absolutely essential to your ability to smooth it in the wilderness. It is your repository for food, fire-making supplies, and health resources, and it furnishes you a place and the materials to build your shelter. Being able to recognize the components of a tree, from the properties of its wood to the medicinal values of its outer leaves and bark, will allow you to take advantage of your environment's largest resource. Recognizing animals and their behavioral patterns is what will help you outthink them when you're hunting. Even the clouds in the sky can provide you with a weather forecast, which you can use to make adjustments to your camp and shelter. Remember to practice! Use short camping trips as an opportunity to hone these skills and experiment with life when you are carrying only a few things. If certain things don't work out right away, that's okay! Head home, rest up, and try it again on your next trip.

This handbook is intended for the woodsman who knows basic primitive survival skills and is looking to advance his knowledge and abilities for a longer stay in the wilderness—a few days or even an entire trapping campaign season. These skills will also help you in the event you become lost or stranded without resources. Mostly, though, these give you a chance to envelop yourself in nature as our ancestors before us did. As George Washington Sears (Nessmuk) wrote, "We seek the forest for adventure and a free, open-air hunter's life, for a time at least." *Advanced Bushcraft* is the handbook for your adventure. Use it to survive and thrive in the natural world.

—Dave Canterbury

Chapter 1
BUILDING YOUR KIT

"The doctorate in woodsy knowledge can only be taught by Mother Nature in the classroom of the outdoors. Many can train you but only experience can teach you."

—DAVE CANTERBURY

Bushcraft is the practice of using wilderness skills to survive and thrive in the natural world. In *Advanced Bushcraft*, you will hone those skills and push beyond the mentality of immediate needs. You will learn to think about the totality of your skills and supplies and how they work together to ensure long-term sustainability. In other words, it's not just about packing resources. It's about thinking ahead to the kinds of skills it takes to refurbish your resources or create more if necessary. You will learn that it takes a lot of skills but only a few tools to become self-reliant. With just a handful of the right implements you can manufacture most of the things you need, from a permanent shelter to clothing, hunting gear, weapons, and even medicine.

PLAN THE SCOPE OF YOUR TRIP

Short-term trips in the woods are great opportunities to practice skills and take chances with a smaller kit. Traveling with fewer implements requires a lot of improvisation with tools and supplies, and it's okay if things do not go perfectly. On a short jaunt, whether it is a day or a week, it does not matter much if your shelter is uncomfortable or if your trapping campaign is not overly successful. Use short-term trips as opportunities for learning and know that if something does not turn out quite right, you can practice again next time to make it better.

A long trip, say a full-season trapping campaign, requires a lot of confidence and certainty in your skills. You do not want to place yourself in a situation of unnecessary risk. For long excursions, a good 4–6 hours of restful sleep each night becomes an imperative component of safety. With that in mind, the comfort level of your shelter and sleeping implements matters a great deal. You might need to bring supplies to trap for food, but you should also plan for a possible unsuccessful trapping campaign by bringing backup food sources. You also need to think about ways to conserve the most valuable resources or make sure that you are not overusing them. It may not be possible to replace a broken knife on the trail.

On a long-term trip, you might also need to include some type of conveyance. Since these are cumbersome, you need to maximize it as a resource. For example, a sled for dragging supplies in the snow can be repurposed to drag firewood or animals from your traps back to camp. Conveyances are not often discussed in bushcraft literature, but they are critical to long-term sustainability. Our ancestors never took to the woods or wilderness without horses, wagons, canoes, sleds, or pack trains.

TEN Cs OF SURVIVABILITY

As discussed in *Bushcraft 101*, the most basic kit items are based on the Five Cs of Survivability. For longer-term stays in the wilderness you can expand that checklist to Ten Cs:

- **Cutting tools:** knives, axes, saws
- **Combustion devices:** ferrocerium rod, lighter, magnifying lens
- **Cover elements:** seasonal clothing with outerwear, tarps, wool blankets, sleeping bag, emergency bivvy, hammock, small tent
- **Containers:** water bottles, canteens, nesting cook pots and pans
- **Cordage:** bankline, paracord, rope, webbing, mule tape
- **Cotton materials:** bandannas, shemagh, netting, cloth shards
- **Cargo tape:** duct tape (I prefer the Gorilla Tape brand)
- **Candling devices:** headlamps, candles, crank lights
- **Compasses:** your preferred brand along with a small backup like a quality button-style
- **Canvas repair needle:** wedge-style needle for repairing heavy materials

Do not forget to include any medications, including something to relieve an allergic reaction, and first-aid kit items.

Now let's break the kit down into categories so that you can really consider your needs.

CORE TEMPERATURE CONTROL

This is the first and most important kit category. Clothing is the most basic way to control temperature. Here are some more specific guidelines:

CLOTHING

Pack at least two full sets of socks and undergarments, trousers, and shirts. Carry clothing that is comfortable in all seasons or be prepared to pack enough clothing for two different climates (for a total of four sets). I would recommend 10–12-ounce durable canvas pants like the tree-climbing pants offered by Arborwear. Long-sleeved, lightweight, canvas, button-down shirts are comfortable in all seasons, and cotton T-shirts take advantage of evaporative cooling in the summer. Do not forget to plan for rain and wet weather. Tentsmiths makes a solid raincoat from cotton treated with an oil/wax finish.

In winter, use a heavy wool layer that will act as insulation, such as the **merino wool pants** offered by Minus33. In general, nothing beats wool in cold-weather climates. It is comfortable, fire retardant, repels moisture, and even when it is wet it still acts as a good insulation. I prefer the Boreal Shirt by Lester River Bushcraft. It has never let me down, even on the coldest of winter days and nights here in the eastern woodlands. If freezing rain and sleet are an issue, combine the wool with an oilcloth raincoat.

FOOTWEAR

Leather boots are an absolute must for long-term wilderness activities. The Pronghorn, from Danner, is a great three-season boot, and their Canadian model works well in the winter. When choosing your footwear, remember that boots are only as waterproof as they are high. Carrying a second pair of boots will save a lot of trouble on long-term trips so you can alternate and avoid wearing them out too quickly. If carrying a second pair is too cumbersome, at least plan to bring a pair of **moccasins** to wear when walking around camp so that you give your boots an occasional rest. Moccasins, elk hide or buffalo, are also handy when stalking game in dry leaves.

HAT

Never underestimate the importance of **hats** when planning your kit. A good hat will protect you from the sun and conserve body heat—most of which is released through the head and the neck. A felted wide-brim hat works well in spring, summer, and fall. A wool beanie or toboggan will help combat the cold in winter. In the most severe weather I have found great comfort in the old leather bomber caps with earflaps and fur linings.

SCARVES

Kerchiefs and **scarves** have been staples of the woodsman's kit for hundreds of years. Their uses go well beyond the obvious. The cotton netting used as a sniper veil works very well in summer and makes a great improvised net for fishing. Kerchiefs made from cotton, like the shemagh, are effective across three seasons. In winter, I prefer a 4' × 4' scarf, which not only keeps me warm but can also be used as a cape to repel snow.

GLOVES AND MITTENS

A sturdy pair of **leather calfskin gloves** will protect the hands from briars, brambles, and blisters when doing normal camp chores. In winter, arctic mittens with wool glove liners are indispensable. I have found that to stay comfortable for a full day on the trail or trap line, keeping my extremities warm is just as important as conserving heat on my core.

TOOLS

When packing tools, what truly distinguishes a sophisticated kit is eliminating redundancies. Let's take a few minutes to discuss different options for critical tools so that you can intelligently decide what to pack in a long-term kit.

FARMED

Remember this acronym when purchasing tools for your kit. It is especially helpful when you are trying to choose between multiple brands and styles:

- Functionality—Is this tool designed for only one specific purpose? Or could it be used to complete several different tasks?
- Affordability—Does this tool fit into my budget, especially when considering the total sum of the tools I need to purchase for my kit?
- Repeatability—Can I perform tasks the same way with this tool and get the same result each time or is there going to be a long learning curve to master it?
- Maintainability—Is this tool easy to maintain over time with a minimum of peripheral gear?
- Ergonomics—Does this tool feel good to me for my body stature and build? Will it tire me easily or cause undue discomfort during use?
- Durability—Is the tool of good quality that will last for years if well maintained?

CHECKLIST OF FIVE MOST IMPORTANT TOOLS

These tools should be the basis of your kit. When deciding which versions of these tools to include in your kit, think about the environmental factors, the type of shelter you plan to build, and the length of your stay:

- Knife
- Axe
- Saw
- Carving tool
- Awl

KNIFE

When you're selecting a knife for your kit, the number of choices can be completely overwhelming. It is a good practice to carry a few knives for different tasks.

BUSHCRAFT TIP	**Three Knives That Are Worth Carrying:** • 5"-6" knife for butchering • Knife for fine carving • Folding knife of high-carbon steel, which can be kept in your pocket

Certain blade profiles are more conducive to certain tasks. A knife with a butchering profile will always be the best overall knife when processing game meat. A slender blade width is better for fine carving tasks, boning, and filleting. If you are building a longer-term kit that includes resources for more advanced tasks in the wilderness, game is going to be a key element to your success. Processing this game for food, tools, and hides is more critical than carving notches so you will need a blade that is specific to this task. A knife for food processing should be about 4"–5" long and fairly thin at about 1/8" or less. A Scandinavian (V) grind will be most useful, but a flat grind is a close second. Both are easily maintained in the

field but are strong enough to act as a primary blade, should
you need a replacement.

Recently there has been much debate over the capabilities of a sheath knife on the hip. Many argue this single tool should be enough to accomplish tasks from fine carving and processing game to splitting firewood. I tend to agree with this philosophy, especially because even if you lose your pack, this knife will always be on your person. Keeping this in mind, be sure to practice using your knife for various tasks before embarking on a long journey.

CARVING TOOLS

In the eastern woodlands, the jackknife, or folding knife, has been considered the best for whittling or fine carving. Morakniv carries a fine line of carving tools. I also like the crooked knife, or mocotaugan, which was a standard carry tool for many native peoples. This knife, similar to the Bent Knife by Deepwoods Ventures, can be used for tasks as versatile as carving canoe paddles to manufacturing replacement handles.

MACHETES AND LONGER BLADES

In many areas of the country a machete may be the best choice of blade in conjunction with a smaller knife. The advantage to the machete is that you can use it to quickly clear a trail or limbs from a tree. It also works as a scraping and crafting tool. In my opinion, the **machete** is truly the "woodsman's pal." Select a size that works best for you, but I find that from the tip of the blade to the base of the handle should be roughly equal to the distance from the elbow to fingertip.

AXE

The main axe you carry should be at least 18"–20" in handle length. A larger axe of 26"–28" in handle length will be much more effective for big tasks such as cutting down large trees. Aside from handle configurations, there are also many head designs and profiles available. An axe with a head weight of up to 3 pounds is good for felling. When selecting an axe, most of the right dimensions come down to personal preference, but whatever you choose, I have found that a good axe is worth its weight in gold on a long trip.

TOMAHAWKS

The **tomahawk**, a personal tool that hangs on the belt, has been used for hundreds of years. It is a backup to a knife. One of the handiest things about the tomahawk is that the handle can be removed so you can use the head alone as a scraping or skinning tool. Tomahawks are too small to process large amounts of firewood or fell large trees, but their handles can be replaced fairly easily if broken, which makes them a good choice for long excursions. There are a lot of tomahawks on the market today, but the ones with heavier heads are most advantageous for wood-processing tasks.

HATCHETS

The decision to carry a tomahawk or a **hatchet** depends on your individual needs and the environment. A smaller crafting-type hatchet can be carried along with the larger axe. Hatchets can be carried right on the belt and are very easy to wield with one hand. They are handy for fine carving and small chopping when processing fire materials. Look for varieties that are designed to put the centerline blade in the proper location when you are choking up on the handle so that it works as a carving or skinning tool as well. Hudson Bay–style heads are great in this application.

SAWS

Folding saws make an excellent addition to your kit as long as the blade is not too aggressive. By aggressive I mean a blade with larger teeth and a wider kerf, or distance between teeth; these do not make fine cuts. It is better to select something with smaller teeth and a narrow kerf. I see many folding saws on the market today with aggressive pruning-type, green-wood blades. The problem with that configuration is that it limits the uses of the saw. A folding saw is most efficient when it doubles as a notch-cutting saw, and for that reason, a crosscutting blade will be much easier to control and your cuts will be cleaner. There are a lot of varieties in the market, but I find the best blade on a folding saw with the best longevity is Bahco's Laplander model.

- **Fixed-blade saws:** These saws include not only crosscutting or dovetail saws but also pruning blades. The types of saws you include in your kit will be dictated by what you plan to do with them. If you are carrying a bucksaw or bow saw that has a green-wood blade, then a simple crosscut blade with a bit finer teeth will be much more desirable than a pruning-type, green-wood blade.
- **Bow Saws and bucksaws (frame saws):** These are safe choices, and their easy use helps to save precious calories. Include one of these in any winter kit, no matter the length of your stay. For longer-term kits, just be sure that the blade is at least 20" long and has both a green-wood and dry-wood blade. The advantage to a bow (metal-frame) saw is durability. I recommend these for long-term outings. Even

though it is made from metal, the frame is actually a hollow tube so the difference in weight is negligible.

AWL

In the trade ledger from the American frontier days, the **awl** was one of the most traded metal items, second only to the knife. Awls are designed to punch holes in materials such as leather, bark, and wood. There are many different types of awls, but the crooked awl is the most versatile. These tools are two-sided with three or four sides to each point. The taper of the awl is usually a little different on opposing ends so that you have some versatility when drilling holes. You can easily fashion a handle for one end of this tool if needed or add a hole for lock-stitch sewing tasks.

COMFORT

In this category you should think about how to get a good night's rest in both long-term and short-term scenarios. Even if you are planning to set up a permanent shelter, you need to be prepared to set up a temporary shelter in case you need to leave base camp for a day or two. A good Egyptian cotton, oilcloth tarp of 8' × 8' minimum, like the one available from Tentsmiths, combined with a moisture barrier such as a tick mattress and a stout woolen blanket will do in the coldest of climates. Just make sure you have a proper bed and fire. The Pathfinder 100 percent wool blanket, from Self Reliance Outfitters, will work as a good three-season blanket, as will Witney (check eBay), Hudson's Bay (available through Woolrich or L.L. Bean), or Tony Baker blankets. You can also look in surplus stores for any blankets that are guaranteed 100 percent wool. Any woolen blanket should be entirely made of wool and should be queen-sized or six-point dimension, approximately 96" × 96".

HAMMOCKS

Hammocks afford many advantages, even for use in a long-term shelter, and give a very comfortable night's sleep. They have been commonly used by woodsmen since the 1800s. Older versions were fashioned from balloon silk, rope netting, or canvas. Balloon silk is not that different in consistency and weight to the parachute-type material used to make hammocks today. Hammocks can be a great three-season option when combined with a blanket. They can even be used in cold weather if you use some kind of quality underquilt that will combat convection issues associated with hanging above ground. A lot of hammock manufacturers now make a bug net that is either built into the hammock or available as an add-on. These nets create a screened enclosure, offering added protection from bugs.

TENTS

Small backpacking-style tents provide comfort and security from bugs and other wigglers. The downside is that their construction restricts your view and eliminates the ability to use fire as a heat source. There is always a tradeoff with any piece of gear! There are a lot of different types of tents on the market, but I would suggest selecting one that is made of the heaviest material you feel comfortable carrying. You will appreciate the durability. One other possible downside to consider is that condensation tends to form inside the tent walls at night, which can make them colder than open shelter. Look for varieties with mesh tops and a rain flap, which helps alleviate the condensation issues.

BIVVIES

A **bivvy** is usually a small tube-style bag that is made for a single person and can be set up very quickly. The same rules apply to bivvies as to tents: Look for durable material with mesh and a closable rain flap to help prevent condensation. Some manufacturers offer bivvies that have a sleeping bag included, like a self-contained sleeping unit.

TENT COTS

There are also tent cots made especially for hunting. These are self-contained tents and sleeping cots built into one unit. They can be quite comfortable and provide all the advantages of a raised bed and closed tent.

ULTRALIGHT COTS

Ultralight cots provide a comfortable raised bed in just a couple of minutes. These cots fold up very small and are extremely light, which makes them a great option for a good night's sleep on longer treks.

> **BUSHCRAFT TIP**
>
> Point blankets are a type of wool trade blanket most associated with the Hudson Bay Company. These old standbys have been sold in North America since 1779. Point blankets have a series of colored lines (points) woven into them on one edge signifying the size of the blanket. During the fur trade era the largest point blanket was a four-point blanket of about 72″ Ð 90″. Modern point blankets can be found up to six points, or approximately 96″ Ð 96″. In today's terms, a four-point blanket would fit a full-sized bed, and a six-point blanket would fit a queen- or king-sized bed. In the old days these points were also used to signify how many finished or "made" beaver hides the blanket was worth. So a six-point blanket was worth the value of six "made" beavers or the equivalent in another fur.

CONVENIENCE

Items of convenience are the lowest priority when building an emergency or survival kit, but in a long-term scenario these items are very important. These are the items that make camp life "smoother" and also add to the longevity of your supplies. They include things that repair and refurbish, candles, navigational aids, extra containers, even snowshoes.

PRIORITIZING ITEMS OF CONVENIENCE

- Repair kits with additional tools
- Premade tinders and fire extenders
- Varied cookware such as folding reflector ovens and skillets
- Additional tarpage for making shelter over work areas
- Additional cordage for major projects like nets

TIPS AND TRICKS

1. Any handled tool should have a handle of wood for ease of replacement in the field.
2. In a pinch, the blade of a bow saw can always be used with a frame saw that you fashion yourself from natural materials such as wood.
3. Save the most precious resources as a last option. For example, never start a fire with a lighter if you can use a ferro rod, and never use a ferro rod if you can use the sun (which is a renewable resource).
4. "Opossum mentality" is always key: Think like a scavenger. Never pass over a needed resource thinking that you will run into it again. This is especially true with materials related to fire, food, or medicine.
5. Any piece of your kit should be versatile enough that it has at least three viable uses.

Chapter 2

NATURAL RESOURCES

"Preconceived notions, especially when one is fairly brought up in their influence, are most difficult to shake off."

—Stewart Edward White, *Camp and Trail*

Natural resources are a critical component of woodcraft and bushcraft. Trees are especially beneficial because they are accessible throughout all four seasons. It's true that some resources within a tree may be better harvested during warmer seasons, but the lumber, roots, and inner bark are always available. There are many trees in the eastern woodlands, and talking about all the specific species is beyond the scope of this book. However, you will learn about some of the most prevalent families of trees, like pine, willow, poplar, oak, and birch, and how to thoroughly use the resources they offer.

BTUS FOR WOOD BURNING

SPECIES	HEAT PER CORD (MILLION BTUS)	% OF GREEN ASH	EASE OF SPLITTING	SMOKE	SPARKS	COALS	FRAGRANCE	OVERALL QUALITY
Black locust	27.9	140	Difficult	Low	Few	Excellent	Slight	Excellent
Black walnut	22.2	111	Easy	Low	Few	Good	Good	Excellent
Bur oak	26.2	131	Easy	Low	Few	Excellent	Good	Excellent
Eastern red cedar	18.2	91	Medium	Medium	Many	Poor	Excellent	Fair
Honey locust	26.7	133	Easy	Low	Few	Excellent	Slight	Excellent
Larch (tamarack)	21.8		Easy-med		Many	Fair	Slight	Fair
Lodgepole pine	21.1		Easy		Many	Fair	Good	Fair
Maple (other)	25.5	128	Easy	Low	Few	Excellent	Good	Excellent
Mulberry	25.8	129	Easy	Medium	Many	Excellent	Good	Excellent
Osage orange	32.9	165	Easy	Low	Many	Excellent	Excellent	Excellent
Ponderosa pine	16.2	81	Easy	Medium	Many	Fair	Good	Fair
Red oak	24.6	123	Medium	Low	Few	Excellent	Good	Excellent
Rocky Mountain juniper	21.8	109	Medium	Medium	Many	Poor	Excellent	Fair
Silver maple	19.0	95	Medium	Low	Few	Excellent	Good	Excellent
Spruce	15.5	78	Easy	Medium	Many	Poor	Slight	Fair
Sycamore	19.5	98	Difficult	Medium	Few	Good	Slight	Good
White oak	29.1	146	Medium	Low	Few	Excellent	Good	Excellent
Willow	17.6	88	Easy	Low	Few	Poor	Slight	Poor

PINE

The pine tree is one of the most abundant trees in the eastern woodlands. It also provides useful resources throughout all four seasons. Since the pine tree is a conifer, it does not lose its needles in the winter when many other tree species drop their leaves. Let's take a closer look at this tree from the outside in to better understand its resources.

Pinewood is fantastic because, due to its resinous nature, it will burn quickly and can be used to make a fire lay even in wet weather. The dark black smoke that you see from a fire made with pine is a product of the resins from within the wood burning off. Pine is a softwood that can make a very effective bow-drill hearth and spindle set—although be careful to avoid the resins or the set will simply polish and not burn. Pine makes a decent carving wood but is not as durable for utensils as other woods.

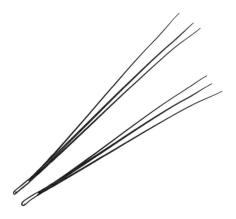

Pine needles

SAP/RESIN

Pine resin is usually found on the outermost part of the tree where an injury has occurred. The dripping or secretion allows you to access and collect something from inside the tree without hurting it. This resin, or **sap**, is like liquid gold and should be collected at any opportunity that presents itself. I carry a separate 4-ounce tin so that I can collect sap anytime I come across it and store it in my kit. As a medicinal resource, pine sap can act like new skin on a shallow cut and generally works as an antiseptic when caring for wounds. The resin itself is highly flammable and is therefore a great flame extender within the fire lay. A very good adhesive, called **pine pitch,** can be made by heating the sap and adding equal parts charcoal and a binder like cattail fluff or herbivore dung. Use a low heat when melting the sap because it becomes very brittle when burned. The resulting glue can then be stored in a tin or wrapped on a **pitch stick** by winding it like cotton candy on a stick and drying it one layer at a time. This stick can later be heated over a fire to soften the glue for application.

NEEDLES

Needles on eastern pines are extremely nutritious and have more vitamin C per weight than a fresh-squeezed orange. Also high in vitamin A, these pine needles make an excellent tea for boosting the immune system. Pine needle tea also works as an expectorant and a decongestant. The tea can even be used as an antiseptic wash or fomentation. Not all pines taste the same, so you should try different types to find what you like best. You can fashion beautiful coil baskets from pine needles, although this task is tedious. Dead pine needles are fantastic additions to any fire lay as the resinous needles are highly flammable. They also make good coarse materials for a bird's nest when making primitive fire.

ROOTS

Certain tree species, such as the spruce, have very long roots that grow just under the surface of the ground. These roots can be harvested in long lengths and used for cord or basket weaving. Once the root is harvested, the outer bark must be removed to make the root more pliable. You can remove the bark by pinching the root between two sticks and pulling the root through, removing the bark as you go. Keep the roots wet so that they are easier to handle. Larger roots can be further split to make the resource last even longer.

FATWOOD

The area of the tree commonly known as the **fatwood** will collect the resins best because it's where the sap settles. Oftentimes the stump and root ball can be an excellent source of fatwood. Not all tree species have a lot of sap, so you will need to experiment with what you have. It is safe to say that *all* pines will contain some fatwood. Many times, a dead standing or fallen tree will have a root ball that is completely saturated with resin. That is the gold mine! If you find yourself in need of an emergency fire-starting device, remember that fatwood is highly flammable. When you combine the accelerant value of resin with the wood as a slow-burning fuel source you have a natural pairing. Choose an area of a living or dead tree where a branch has grown and cut the branch as close to the trunk as possible. Here you will find at least a few inches of fatwood. To process this wood for starting a fire, locate the dark, orange-colored fatwood area and scrape this into fine shavings with the back of your knife. This material will ignite with an open flame or a ferrocerium rod.

INNER BARK

The inner bark can be used as a food source. It also holds many antiseptic properties and can even be used as an impromptu bandage. When dried, the inner bark can also be used to make slats for woven baskets.

WILLOW

Willow is a water indicator tree, since it only grows well in wet areas along river and stream banks, drainage areas, and lakesides. Willow wood is soft, good for carving, and one of the best materials for a hearth and spindle when making a bow-drill fire set.

Willow leaf

LEAVES AND BRANCHES

Willow leaves and the inner bark contain salicin, which is one of the chemical compounds used in aspirin. A decoction of the inner bark will make a fairly good headache remedy, and chewing the leaves will alleviate a toothache.

The branches of the willow grow long, and new growth is fairly straight, which is why they make passable arrow shafts. Willow branches are pliable and can therefore be used to make quick basket containers as well.

INNER BARK

Willow's inner bark can be used to make baskets and pack boards. The bark is best harvested in the spring and early summer when the bark is loose and can easily be pried from the tree with a wedge. The outer bark can then be separated by peeling the inner bark from it. As with most of these types of components, the inner bark is most workable when kept wet.

POPLAR

There are many poplars in the eastern woodlands. The tulip poplar (sometimes known as the yellow poplar) is one of my favorites, but it is actually a magnolia and not a true poplar. Daniel Boone's canoe was carved from this wood. The poplar is a soft tree and therefore makes an excellent primitive fire set such as a bow drill. The poplar makes a fine spindle as well as a hearth board for this purpose. Also fine for carving, it makes easy small camp items like spoons and spatulas.

Tulip Poplar leaf

LEAVES

The leaves and the barks of this tree are very astringent and can be used medicinally for drawing infection or for driving toxins, like the oils from poison ivy, to the surface. A hot fomentation combined with a wash is one of the best ways to rid your skin of the ivy oils that cause rash. When taken as an infusion, the leaf tea is binding and can relieve diarrhea.

OUTER BARK

During the spring, easily remove the outer bark by prying it from the sapwood with a wedge or your axe blade. You can use this bark to make bark containers from baskets to arrow quivers. To do this, make two circular cuts through the bark around the tree; the distance between the cuts should be the desired length of the piece. Then, to open the bark, make a vertical cut by inserting a wedge between the bark and sap. You can then slowly peel off the outer bark. Remember that peeling off the bark will kill the tree, so make sure it is absolutely necessary before you do it.

INNER BARK

In the eastern woodlands, the inner bark of the poplar is one of the most prized resources next to pine sap. The inner bark provides both bird's nest material and tinder bundles for fire. When harvested green, it also makes a strong reverse wrap for two-ply cordages. Many times the inner bark fibers can easily be seen through rotting bark hanging off the branches. If branches are dead but not shedding, the back of your knife will easily process this to make the inner bark accessible.

OAK

The oak, with its heavy grain and hard wood, has tradition-ally been used for construction. Oak is excellent for crafting wooden tools and even replacement handles for tools. There are two major groups of oaks: red oak and white oak.

- **Red oak** is great for any building materials like slat boards and dimensional lumber. Red oak is a fibrous wood that handles bending stress easily, so it can also be used for making bows. Red oak can be used to heat-form many supplies such as pack frames and snowshoe frames.
- **White oak** represents the medicinal side of the oak family. In medieval times, the white oak leaf was the symbol for materia medica, that is, the collected knowledge about medicines and the conditions they were used to treat. The inner bark of white oak can help relieve sinus congestion and headaches. Due to the high level of tannins, the leaves and the barks of this tree are very astringent and can be used for drawing infection or for driving things to the surface, like the oils from poison ivy, and for relieving diarrhea. White oak is antiseptic in nature, so decoctions of this bark make excellent mouthwashes and gargles for sore throat or gum problems.
- **Oak wood** is a long-burning hardwood, which makes it a great choice for all-night fires and for creating coal beds in cook fires.

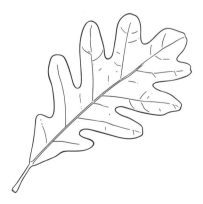

Oak leaf

SASSAFRAS

I include sassafras here because of the carminative value of the root tea. Finely ground dry sassafras leaves will also add a cinnamon-type flavor to foods such as bannock, a quick-fry bread. Sassafras was a mainstay tonic from colonial times until the 1960s when the FDA conducted tests that showed mass amounts of safrole caused liver cancer in rats. Root decoction can be used to ease upset stomach and regulate the digestive system.

Sassafras leaf

BIRCH

There are several species of birch throughout the eastern woodlands, but black and river birch are the most prevalent in the middle ground areas of the Ohio River valley. All birches contain oil that can be extracted from the bark, and it is so flammable that it can often still burn even when damp. Birch is an excellent carving wood and is the preferred material for Scandinavian-made knife handles.

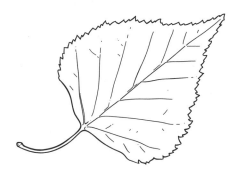

Birch leaf

BIRCH BARK

Birch bark provides probably the most versatile and even life-saving resources of all the trees in the eastern woods, save maybe the pine. With its rich and volatile oils, birch bark burns with a dark black smoke that in the summer can help drive off insects. It is virtually unmatched in its ability to burn in damp conditions, and when using open flame it requires almost no processing to quickly create a hot, warming fire while drying marginal tinder as it goes. Birch bark is also prized as a material for crafting containers of all sorts and for weaving to make baskets and sheaths. Native peoples used birch bark to make the outer skin of canoes. It is best to harvest the bark from live trees between May and June, but this tree is so resilient and resistant to rot that bark can even be harvested from dead trees. It is possible to harvest the outer bark without killing a live tree as long as you are able to do so without disturbing the inner bark. Make test cuts to determine the thickness and pliability of the bark before making large harvests.

CHAGA (TINDER FUNGUS)

Birches that grow at higher altitudes or in colder climates are susceptible to a parasitic fungus commonly called tinder fungus (*Inonotus obliquus*), or chaga. Chaga grows in areas of the United States from New England and Michigan down to North Carolina. Chaga has long been sought for both its medicinal and fire tinder properties. It appears as a large blackened ball or mass on the side of the trunk of both live and fallen birch. This fungus has extensive medicinal value; many woodsmen will simply boil a chunk of it in their kettle as a daily tea to drink at camp. When it's used as a fire starter, the yellow soft areas beneath the black outer crust will take the sparks from both steel and rod and will hold an ember to be used for ignition. You can slice it thinly or create a dust that can then be stored in your kit for later use.

MEDICINAL VALUE OF TREE RESOURCES	
TREE	MEDICINAL VALUE
Pine	Decongestant, antiseptic, immune system booster
Willow	Pain reliever
Poplar	Astringent, diarrhea relief
Oak	Decongestant, astringent, diarrhea relief
Sassafras	Regulate digestive system
Birch	Antiseptic, insect repellant

BIRCH OIL

Birch oil is extracted by using two containers of metal or clay. The first, called the **catchment container,** is buried below ground to the rim and surrounded by dirt. The second container is filled with birch bark and sealed with a drain hole or holes in the bottom from which oil drains into the catchment container. This container is placed just over the catchment container. A fire is then built around the aboveground container to heat the material and release the oils until they slowly drain into the container below. The process usually takes several minutes to fill a small container. Then the top container is carefully removed to expose the pool of oil below. This oil is highly medicinal and can be used as both an antiseptic and an insect repellant. It is also flammable, so be cautious when using it.

> **BUSHCRAFT TIP**
>
> Birch oil can be further rendered into birch tar. To create birch tar you will need to slowly heat the oil to a boil like a gravy and then stir. Be careful because both the fumes and the liquid are highly flammable. Once rendered to a thick paste it can be rolled onto a stick where it can be stored for later use. This form of storage is called a **pitch stick.** The tar can also be molded onto squares or balls for storage and later use. Birch tar can be used for many purposes. When reheated, it is a completely waterproof gluing material. It is also a flexible adhesive and can be used for hafting and sealing both containers and leathers such as moccasin seams.

ITEMIZE

It's true that plants and trees provide many resources, but it is absolutely critical that they are identified correctly before using them. A friend of mine, Green Dean, teaches a simple method for this called ITEM:

- I—Properly Identify the plant with at least two resources.
- T—Consider the Time of year: Is the plant growing or blooming in the proper season for its species?

- E—Observe the Environment: Is the plant or tree growing in a location true to its nature? For example, a plant that prefers dry, rocky soil will likely not be found in a marsh.
- M—Research the Method of harvest and preparation. Many plants must be harvested at a certain time in their life cycle, or a certain part must be harvested for use. Find out what method is used to prepare this plant for food or medicine. Does it need to be leached? Does it need to be double boiled to create a decoction?

MEDICINAL PREPARATIONS

Here are some basic methods used to prepare natural resources for medicinal use:

- **Infusion**—This process is just like making tea. The portions of the plant to be used are placed in water that has already been boiled and removed from the fire. A lid is placed on the container and the mixture is left to steep for 15–30 minutes. It is then consumed as needed.
- **Decoction**—Similar to the way you make an infusion, you are going to boil water. With a decoction, however, you will add the bark or roots to the boiling water while it is still on the fire and simmer until half the liquid remains. Then add water to the original amount again and repeat. Once you have essentially twice-boiled the liquid, it can be strained and consumed or used as needed. Note: This method is always used for extraction from bark and roots.
- **Fomentation**—A fomentation is an infusion or decoction in which a cotton material has been steeped for about 5 minutes and is then wrapped or placed on the skin.

- **Wash**—You use a wash of either an infusion or decoction to wash or irrigate an area. You can also possibly soak something in it, such as your feet.
- **Poultice**—A poultice is usually the macerated plant wrapped against the skin with a bandage. This method is used mainly for drawing or to reduce swelling.

TIPS AND TRICKS

1. If you are having problems identifying a tree in the winter months when you have only the bark to examine, look on the ground around the tree. The leaves around it, even if dry, will be a good indicator of what type of tree it is.
2. When using tree bark as a resource, remember that the birch is the only tree that you can ring or girdle without killing the entire tree.
3. After injuring a tree, applying a fresh coat of thick mud will help to protect it from further damage as it heals.
4. Always collect "punky" wood, which is wood that is nearly rotten and very spongy in appearance and feel. Punky wood makes the charred material for the next fire.
5. Keep an eye out for water vines. In an emergency, if water is unavailable, wild grape or water vines will hold water for several months from early spring through summer. Cut the vine close to the ground first and then about 2' higher. A large vine will hold up to a cup of water.

Chapter 3

WOODEN TOOLS
AND SIMPLE MACHINES

"Nature's Priority: Take care of the brain first. Then it will take care of you."

—Gene Fear,
Surviving the Unexpected Wilderness Emergency

In addition to the five critical metal tools discussed in Chapter 1, there are five wooden tools you can easily craft yourself to aid in a long-term outing. The selection is dependent on the type of trip you have planned and what food and meat procurement supplies you are carrying. This list takes into consideration the fact that you are crafting most of your tools as you go in order to keep down the weight of your kit. This is especially true when you are traveling without conveyances.

THROWING OR DIGGING STICK

The first thing I usually make while preparing my camp is a **throwing stick,** which can also be used for digging. Although this type of tool is one of the easiest to make, it adds a lot of versatility to your kit. The throwing stick should be made of green hardwood (oak, maple, magnolia) if possible and is about the length from your armpit to your cupped hand, or what I call "axe-handle length." I cut a 45° wedge on one end and a dull point on the other. This simple tool can be tucked into the back of your belt or bedroll until needed. You now have a ready tool to throw at game on the ground such as rabbits and squirrels, and you can also use it to dig fire-pit holes or uproot plants and tubers. It can be used as a ready baton if needed for processing firewood or even for retrieving hanging deadwood by tying a string to it, throwing it over a branch, and pulling. The most beautiful thing about this multifunctional tool is it only takes about 2 minutes to manufacture and is therefore easy to replace.

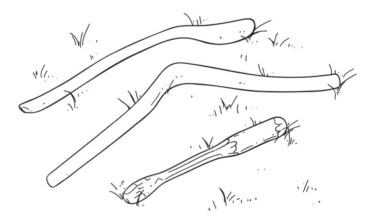

Throwing stick

ANVIL STUMP

Find a large stump if you can, or just cut off a piece of log that is large enough for a seat. You will be surprised at the many uses it will afford over a short time. This stump will keep you off the ground and will also function as a workbench and a dry surface on which to process fire tinder and kindling. The anvil stump can also be used much like a sawhorse when you add V notches on the side into which you can place pieces of wood that need to be cut. Just lay your stump on its side and lock the piece of wood you want to cut into the V notch. The wider the notch, the bigger the piece of wood you can lay into it. This will help you avoid driving your axe or knife into the dirt by accident. The anvil stump provides a raised surface for a candle at night as well. The anvil stump can be further processed to make a grinding bowl on the surface and, on the other side, a series of cutouts that can be used to hold sharpening stones and flats of wood that can be used for cutting boards.

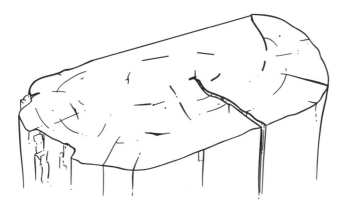

Anvil stump (clave)

SPEAR OR GIG

The **spear**, simple as it may sound, is extremely useful for a variety tasks when you are roaming. It should be constructed of a hardwood sapling like maple and should be at least 12" taller than eye level when finished. Make a stout fork that has about 4" tines on one end. The other end can be fashioned in one of two ways depending on the environment. If you are close to a good water source, such as a flowing steam or pond, you will want a gigging device on the other end. Make this gig by splitting the end of the sapling in a cross fashion to create four equal tines, each of which are about 6"–8" long. Then sharpen the stick as if it were still one solid piece. After this, two small green sticks will be placed into the crosscuts to force open the tines. You can then lash the stick to keep it from splitting further before sharpening the individual tines.

Once this is completed you have a tool that can be used for hunting things like frogs, fish, snakes, and small mammals in dens. This tool will also give you reach to retrieve nuts or nests from high points in trees. Use your spear for stability by using it as a third leg when crossing streams. You can also use it as a support for hanging a pot over the fire if needed. You will find infinite uses for this simple tool as you travel and hunt.

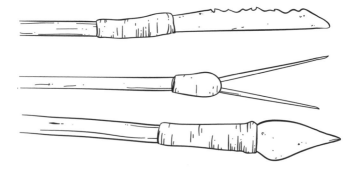

Spear

MAUL OR MALLET

A **maul** can be easily fashioned from a cut green hardwood branch. Mauls vary in size, but I would start with a branch that is approximately 16" long and 4" in diameter. Carve the head from the first 6" of the branch and reduce the other end of the cut wood so that it comfortably fits in the hand, making its weight forward like a large, round hammer. This tool can be used for many tasks, especially for striking the back of a metal tool such as your knife or your axe. This tool will transform your axe into a wedge, a chisel, or a sheer cutting device with more control than if you are just swinging it freely. The maul can also be used to baton wood with your knife if the need arises. Finally, you can easily open or smash acorns, nuts, and clam shells with this tool. Because the maul has a larger surface area than the hammer pole on your axe, it's also a great device for driving wooden stakes and wedges.

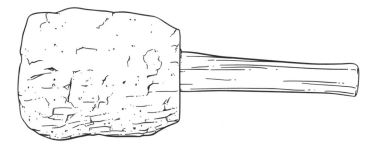

Maul

WEDGES

As soon as you need to split wood, you will need to make **wedges**. If you are forced to use a knife for processing wood, a wedge can be vitally important to safely remove a knife that gets stuck during a split. Wedges should be made from green hardwood material and, as with most of these tools, should be made in varying diameters and angles. Wedges can also be used for splitting longer logs to make things like bow staves or dimensional lumber. They're also useful for separating bark from sapwood to make containers or bark shingles for roofing materials. When not in use, wedges can double as tent stakes. For that reason alone, I recommend fashioning six separate wedges about 1"–2" in diameter and at least 12" long. In this way, these tools become one of the five simple machines you use most often in the woods.

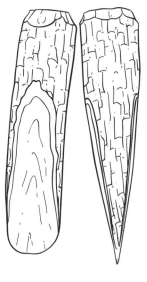

Wedge

SIMPLE WOODLAND MACHINES

Aside from wedges, there are four other simple machines that you can fashion from wood material found in the landscape to help with tasks in and around camp.

WINDLASS

The **windlass** is used to move heavy weights or for tensioning. Typically, a windlass consists of a horizontal cylinder that is rotated by the turn of a crank or belt. A winch is affixed to one or both ends and a cable or rope is wound around the winch, pulling a weight attached to the opposite end. A windlass can be made even more simply with a loop of cord or rope anchored to a fixed object and then looped around another object to be moved. A lever of proportionate size is then placed within the loop and turned, end over end, to tighten the line until it eventually moves the object.

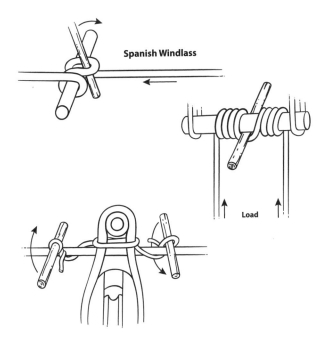

Windlass operation #1

You can also use larger posts as levers, either at ground level or standing, winding rope to move an object. A windlass can also be as simple as a tensioning device for a bucksaw, made from natural materials. A quick vise can be made from a green stump by employing a windlass to tension the work piece. A windlass operates very similar to a tourniquet in this case. It employs a few wraps of rope tensioned by a stick that is then held in place by tying it off to the lower area of the stump. It acts to constrict the work piece and as a holdfast. Killing-type traps sometimes also include a windlass device.

Windlass operation #2

INCLINED PLANE

An **inclined plane** is a simple machine for moving heavy objects above ground. The inclined plane takes advantage of angles in order to lever or pull weight forward on a shallow angle. This makes it easier to lift than pulling dead weight directly from the ground. You can, for example, move a larger log onto a bucking horse or pull a log uphill. To operate the inclined plane you take advantage of the hill and the log as a cylindrical rolling object. From there, you use a windlass to control the task of raising the log uphill.

To pull a log uphill you will take advantage of the incline plane of the hillside. You will need a length of rope long enough to form a W with the center wrapped around a tree at the top of the hill and the two outside Vs wrapping the log. The tails on the outside are used at the top to roll the log up the hill, with two people pulling at the same time.

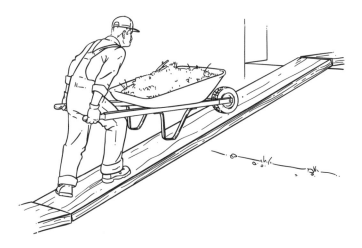

Inclined plane

LEVER AND FULCRUM

A **lever** made of strong material like green hardwood can be used not only to roll large logs and stones across the ground but also to assist in rolling logs up an inclined plane. When using a fulcrum in conjunction with a lever, you can also lift logs and other heavy objects.

BOW AND DRILL

The **bow and drill** is one of the oldest simple machines. It is used as a primitive fire starter and can also be used in conjunction with bits of metal or stone to make holes in other objects. You'll need to create a chuck when using this device for anything other than fire making. (Sometimes chucks are used for making fire too.) For more on this machine see the following chapter.

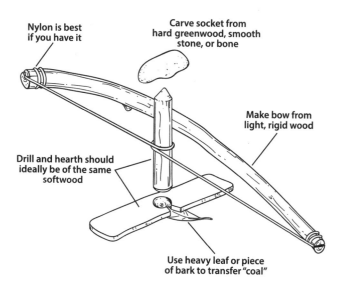

Bow and drill

TIPS AND TRICKS

1. In the long run you will want dry wood for constructing many tools and handles, so collect good, straight hardwood pieces ahead of time so they have time to dry out completely around camp.

2. Wood will dry out and crack faster once the bark is removed. This can be both an advantage and disadvantage, depending on the project for which you are collecting wood. You may want the wood to form a crack, which will make it easier to split.

3. Always hang on to the shavings and materials you collect during woodworking projects. Store them in a dry place so they can act as ready tinder for fire starting later.

4. Heavy cordage such as rope is one of the hardest things to reproduce from natural material, so this asset will always be a priority for longer-term kits.

5. Any wooden tool will need to be oiled to keep it from drying out over time. Use animal fats or birch oil for this task. When a wooden tool is first made, you should oil it least every day for a week, every week for a month, and every month for a year.

— Chapter 4 —
ADVANCED FIRECRAFT

"To poke a wood fire is more solid enjoyment than almost anything else in the world."
—CHARLES DUDLEY WARNER

Fire is the resource that many bushcrafters consider only second in importance to a good cutting tool. Fire is critical for preventing cold-weather injury and providing general comfort around camp in cold environments. Fire can also be used to disinfect water, cook and preserve food, prepare medicines, and keep bugs at bay. There are probably a hundred uses for fire that can contribute to all four categories of your kit (temperature control, tools, comfort, and conveniences). Building fire in an emergency should be easy for a seasoned woodsman. There are plenty of items on the market today, from lighters to road flares, that will almost ensure a flame can ignite even marginal tinder sources.

PRIMITIVE FIRE STARTING

As mentioned in the Ten Cs of Survivability, you should have three items for ignition in supply at all times:

1. Lighter
2. Ferrocerium rod
3. Magnification lens (sunglass)

Beyond these methods of emergency fire starting there are a number of primitive methods that woodsmen have been using for ages. What distinguishes these methods is that you will be using an ember to ignite tinder materials. There are five fire-starting methods in which every woodsman should be competent: open flame (lighter), ferrocerium rod, magnification lens, flint and steel, and bow and drill. These will ensure that the woodsman is prepared and can be comfortable, or "smooth it," in a woodland environment. Matches are not included in this list because I do not believe they add anything to what the first methods can accomplish, especially considering the issues that can encumber their use like moisture, wind, and loss of gross motor dexterity in cold weather. Keep matches in your kit, though, to be used in conjunction with any other method of ignition—just in case.

The two most important primitive methods of fire starting to understand are:

1. Bow and drill
2. Flint and steel

Both of these methods use material from the landscape and your high-carbon blade. The bow and drill kit can be made with your stone or glass tools, but a knife makes the job much more convenient. Some would tell you that to truly practice a primitive skill you must always use primitive tools.

The truth is, in modern society it is easy to find metal and glass materials to use.

THE BOW AND DRILL METHOD

You will use your bow-drill kit to create an **ember**, a smoldering coal to add to a bird's nest of combustible materials. The ember is a critical component of the bow-drill kit because you cannot make fire without it.

To create fire you need three key elements known as the **triangle of fire**: heat, oxygen, and fuel. To create the smoldering coal, your set must take maximum advantage of all three. Methods in survival are like processes of manufacturing in that all inputs will affect the output. It is crucial that you ensure many things happen—and in the correct order—so that you get the desired output.

The bow and drill set has four components:

1. Spindle or drill
2. Hearth board
3. Bearing block
4. Bow

Used correctly, these components work as a simple machine that removes material and causes a fine dust to accumulate. The dust is then heated by the drill's friction at which point oxygen in the surrounding air will allow ignition. Choosing the correct components, using the right form, and understanding when and how much pressure and speed to apply are the key inputs to this process. The only variation should be in the resources you select.

SPINDLE

Make the **spindle** from a softwood so that when you push down on it your fingernail leaves an impression. Poplars, cedars, willows, and pines are all good woods to use. The spindle only needs to be about the same diameter as your thumb and the length from your outstretched thumb to pinky. Since you will be carving both ends, it is okay if it is even a little bit longer.

The spindle needs to be as straight and round as possible. If your wood piece is slightly crooked or bent, use the back of your knife to carefully shave it a little at a time until it is straight. Next it is time to prepare the ends for use. One end of the drill should look like a worn eraser on a pencil: slightly rounded but still basically flat. This end will be placed on the hearth board to create maximum surface area and friction. You want all the friction between the spindle and the hearth to be in this spot. The top of the spindle needs to be shaped like the lead side of a pencil: a pointed shape but slightly dull. Make sure there is very little friction at the top of the spindle so that you can push and pull the bow easily.

Spindle

HEARTH BOARD

The **hearth board** should be made from the same softwood as the spindle. The wood should be dry but not in a state of decay. I prefer to use wood from the tulip poplar because the lower branches often hang dead from the tree and, barring a hard rain, are able to dry out above ground. You will want your finished hearth board to be about as long as your forearm and as thick as your thumb. Select a limb or piece of wood larger than what you need so that you can split it down to make a flat board with these dimensions.

Careful construction of the hearth board and the notch, which must be made correctly in order to achieve a collection of material for a coal while gathering enough oxygen for ignition, is the most important step. Make a small divot in a spot on the hearth. Where you make this initial starting point is dependent on whether you are left- or right-handed, as part of the board will be under your foot. Just make sure the divot is not too close to the end as that may cause the board to split or break out under pressure. A good starting point would be about 2" from the end closest to your dominant hand. You do not need make this divot very deep; it only needs to guide the spindle during the burning process.

BEARING BLOCK

The **bearing block** is a key part of the set but is probably the least understood and the most complicated to start. It should be made from the hardest wood available, such as hickory or beech. Softwoods quickly start to wear away, which causes the spindle to rub on the angled areas below the point. This common mistake is called **shouldering out**, and it will leave the operator exhausted and inhibit the set from running smoothly. Select a green sapling that is about 3" in diameter and cut out a 4"–5" piece on the widest end. Then split one-third off the sapling using your knife.

> As mentioned, the bearing block is the most difficult item to produce, and it controls everything. In general, any hard, natural material makes a good block as long as a divot can be carved into it. Rocks, bones, and antler will all work.

Use your knife to create a small divot on the flat side of this block, right in the middle. The divot only needs to be large enough to accept the point of the spindle. A free-spinning drill will be easy to operate. If you are having problems with your setup, the spinning drill is the first place to double-check.

Bearing block

BOW

The bow can be made from any branch and does not have to necessarily be bent like a bow, but it needs to be fairly stiff so that it does not break under strain. The bow should be about 3' long and ½" in diameter. The longer the bow, the fewer the number of strokes it will take to make the revolutions of the spindle. A common mistake is to use a bow well under 3'.

Making the bow is as simple as tying a string to a branch. There are many complicated notches and holes you can create to string the bow, but I have found that a simple fork on one end of the stick with a loop and a stake notch on the other end to tie it off with a straight lashing and a clove hitch works best. The string does not need to be so tight that it causes the bow to bend in order to load the spindle, but the string cannot be so loose that the drill slips under downward pressure.

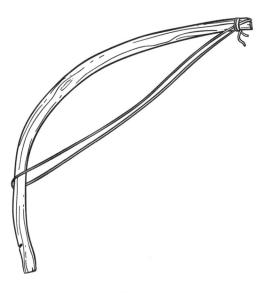

Bow

THE BIRD'S NEST

The ember that you ignite with your bow and drill will be used to ignite a **bird's nest,** a key part of your fire lay. The bird's nest must be made up of coarse, medium, and fine materials. In fact, most of the materials you gather to make the hearth and spindle can also be used when assembling the bird's nest. The inner barks of the poplar or willow, or bark from the cedar, all work well. There are lots of other items that can be used in the bird's nest: for instance, small dead pine needles and materials with a natural accelerant or highly combustible oils like birch bark. Be careful not to use too much dry grass and leaves because these items burn quickly and it is important that the bird's nest burn long enough to ignite the rest of the fire lay materials.

Bird's nest

Processing Material for the Bird's Nest

Processing is the task of shredding barks to amass a quantity of fine material. It is the most important task in constructing the bird's nest. Make sure you place something to catch the shreds so that they do not fall onto the ground. If the material you are collecting is still attached to the tree, you can use the back of your knife to process the shavings. If the material you are collecting is wet, process it immediately and spread it out over a larger surface so that it will dry quickly. You can place some of this processed material between layers in the cloths around the core body area to dry them or spread them out on a dark surface (like a tarp) in the sun. Once the material is dry it can be fashioned to look like a bird's nest. If you come across a bird's nest in the wild, take a look at how it is constructed. When building their nests, birds place fine material in the middle or center and add progressively coarser material as they work their way to the outside. Remember the best bird's nest for a fire lay is an actual bird's nest, so be sure to collect one if you find it available and unoccupied.

BURNING THE HOLE AND MAKING THE NOTCH

Now that the components of your bow drill are ready, it is time to get started. First load the spindle onto the bow. Place the spindle on the divot on the hearth board. Set yourself up with the correct form: Make sure your wrist is locked into your shin in order to prevent the spindle from moving side to side. Make sure there are no obstructions that will interfere with the full movement of the bow. Lean forward to push steady downward pressure on the spindle with the bearing block. Your chest should be over your knee. Begin to apply enough downward pressure with the bearing block to hold the drill in the divot as you slowly rotate the spindle. It is important that you move slowly because this step will marry the drill to the divot for when you begin to create the coal. If you use the entire bow with steady strokes, downward pressure will create enough friction to begin burning the wood. Stop once the wood has burned around the spindle and things are running smoothly because using too much of the material now reduces what you have to make a coal.

Next you need to make a notch from the center of the freshly burned divot hole to the edge of the hearth board. The notch must be made correctly in order to achieve a collection of material for a coal while gathering enough oxygen for ignition. You always want the notch to the front of the board facing away from you because this will allow you to easily view the process when operating the drill. Take care that your notch area is not too narrow, which would cause it to clog up, prevent overspill, and limit oxygen to the ember. Alternately, make sure the burned divot hole is not too big because the dust needs to be compact and the oxygen controlled. A proper notch should be in a V cut in which the bottom of the V goes approximately ⅛ the size of your burned divot circle into the blackened area. The angles of the V should be between 30°–45°.

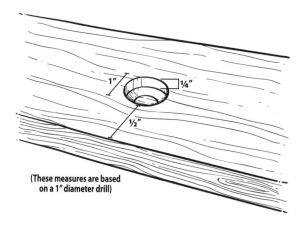

(These measures are based on a 1″ diameter drill)

Constructing the bow drill

MAKING AN EMBER

Now that you've burned your spindle hole and made your notch, inspect each component carefully before attempting to make a coal. Any issues at this point will only get worse later.

1. Check the bowstring for stretch and retighten if necessary.
2. Check the bearing block to make sure the divot is not getting too deep and that the spindle has not begun to shoulder out.

Now you are ready to begin making fire with sticks! There is one extra, small task that makes things easier and might save a good coal from going out due to ground moisture. You need to make a **welcome mat**, a place for your coal to flow onto once it is created in the notch. The welcome mat can be a small sliver of bark or a thin piece of wood that is about two times as wide as the notch. This piece will go under the hearth board to catch the coal.

Operate the bow slowly at first to establish and maintain a rhythm. Your chest should be over your knee so that you can easily observe the activity in the notch. You don't need speed yet; you want steady, long strokes that use the entire length of the bow while you exert downward pressure. At this point the goal is to remove material from the board and the drill and fill the notch with dark brown fluff. Many folks make the mistake of moving too fast, assuming speed will make an ember, but the fact is, if there is no dust in the notch, you have no fuel to create the ember.

After several strokes you will begin to see smoke and the notch will start to fill with material. Once the material in the notch begins to spill forward in front of the notch you can increase the cadence of your bow strokes by about two to three times; it should only take about 10–12 full strokes of the bow at this point to create a burning coal. Stay steady and make sure you do not make a jerky stop that might disturb the coal you created. Slow down during the last couple strokes and stop in the same position you started. Slowly remove the spindle and bow and observe the coal. If it seems to be smoking outside the board where the dust has gathered, you are probably home free. Don't get too excited though, because you still have a lot of time left in the process, probably about 5 or more minutes. Slowly lift the board at an angle and tap it gently with the spindle to dislodge any material that might be clogged in the notch. If the coal is still smoking at this point, you can sit back and relax for a minute, catch a few breaths, and smile!

USING THE COAL TO IGNITE THE BIRD'S NEST

Now comes the most important part of the equation. Always bring the bird's nest to the coal—never the other way around. Make any necessary adjustments to your bird's nest to make sure there is plenty of fine combustible material in the middle. Tilt the nest toward the welcome mat and pick up the welcome mat, moving it toward the nest. Then slowly tap the welcome mat to dump the coal into the nest. This should only be a ¼" drop at most! Slightly fold the nest and begin to add some oxygen by breathing into it slightly, not hard blows just light breaths. If the coal is still burning strongly, you can tilt the nest slightly so that you are blowing up into it, causing the heat to rise into the bulk of the nest. As the ember grows, smoke will begin to roll from the back of the nest, which is the cue for you to blow a bit harder. As the smoke thickens you can increase the oxygen until it begins to burn. Once the nest starts to flame, turn it over so the flames are on the bottom and heat rises to the nonburning material. Finally, place it into your fire lay and make a fire!

FLINT AND STEEL METHOD

The **flint and steel method** is important for you to understand for the same reason you need to know the bow and drill method: in case some kind of emergency causes you to lose the majority of your gear. As long as you do not lose your primary cutting tool of high-carbon steel, you should be able to find a rock in most regions that will drive material from the back of your blade and help achieve this method of ignition. It may take some searching to find a rock that will work for this task, but generally any flint, chert, or quartz rock will work if you can break or find a sharp edge.

For this method you will need to drive small shards of iron material from the back of your knife with a rock. These particles will combust with friction and oxygen at 800°F. Why is this important? Remember, if you need to make a bow-drill fire, it is because you have lost the majority of your kit. You want to avoid having to make two bow-drill fires if you can help it, so you make charred material as soon as you have set the first fire.

MATERIAL FOR FLINT AND STEEL IGNITION

The best way to ensure an easier fire after the bow drill is to have charred materials ready for the next time around so a flint-and-steel fire can be made instead. Some funguses such as chaga (true tinder fungus) will take the spark from this method without having to char it first. You can also get the dust from some types of shelf fungus (*Fomes fomentarius*) to accept a spark. To accomplish this you will require a small pile of dust that you have created with a saw cut or by scraping with the back of the knife. Once the dust has ignited it must be left to grow into a coal, whereas the true tinder fungus can be ignited within a larger piece and the dust is not necessary. With either, you want to use the softer, inner materials, not the outer, hard surface.

An alternative is char material, which even better ensures a spark for ignition. Char can be made from many things you find in the landscape, including punky, decaying wood or the inner pith from some plants like mullein. You can also use materials that are 100 percent cotton from clothing or your kit.

Making Char

The easiest way to make char is to place your chosen material in a metal chamber where you can subject it to high heat while limiting oxygen. In this chamber, gases are able to escape as the material is heated inside. A stainless-steel bottle and nesting cup will work nicely, or even in an emergency an old can with a flat rock. Place your material inside the chamber and then place the chamber in the fire. Coals are better than direct flame but either will work. As the material is heated, smoke—which is actually gas—will begin to escape the chamber from any place that is not completely sealed. This is okay just so long as oxygen cannot enter the chamber. Once the smoke stops, the charring should be complete. It is very important to wait until the chamber is completely cool before opening it because if oxygen contacts hot material it will cause it to burn.

BUSHCRAFT TIP

There are many advantages to making char material. For one, char is highly combustible, so adding it to the marginal materials within a bird's nest gives an extended heat source for effecting ignition. In fact, charred material can be ignited with almost any spark from old lighters, ferrocerium rods, or a sunglass. Given its variety of ignition methods, char is an important material to keep in good supply in your kit.

Inspect the char. If it is black and frail looking, it is most likely ready. If the material is brown, close the chamber and put it back into the fire. You can also test a small amount of the char to make sure it is ready. Many woodsmen carry a specific container such as an Altoids tin or an old shoe polish can, called a char tin, for fire material and charring. Strike sparks from the metal tool directly into the tin, which increases the surface area for catching an ember. Once an ember is created, place it into the bird's nest as described for the bow-drill fire.

SOLAR FIRE

There is a huge advantage to using a **sunglass** to create an ember. Since the sun is a renewable resource, you are not expending anything from your kit when you use it. All the materials for making an ember can be collected from the wild and are not difficult to use. A sunglass can ignite any char material or either of the fungus species previously mentioned—which can be used in a raw state, often straight from the tree for this method. Horse hoof fungus may work better as a dust, but it will make a nice coal in a short amount of time. You can also create an ember by compressing natural materials like cattail down or poplar barks into a small, tight ball about ¼" in diameter. Then use the glass to burn into the material, creating a smoldering ember.

A WORD ON MATCHES

Matches have been the standby for starting fires for more than 150 years, but they really should just be carried as an extra resource in addition to the three main ignition sources: a lighter, a large ferrocerium rod, and a sunglass. Matches are extremely sensitive to weather and moisture, and you can only carry so many. It would take several boxes of matches to come close to the open-flame power and longevity of a single BIC cigarette lighter. The one small advantage of matches may be the tiny amount of tinder a wooden match requires, but this is negligible in a proper fire lay. Many institutions still teach lighting fires with matches, but I believe this method contributes nothing toward true long-term survivability in the wilderness.

ADVANCED BUSHCRAFT TIP

Most softwood species can be scraped with the back of the knife to create fine shavings for ignition with an open flame or a ferrocerium rod. Inner barks and barks of things like cedar, poplar, grape vine (water vine), and honeysuckle will make a combustible nest if dry. Fatwood is the woodsman's sure fire, and it works well even in the dampest conditions. Fine scrapings and shavings of resinous fatwood pine will ignite easily and burn long enough to catch marginal tinder sources. Birch bark, which contains a volatile oil, will also be highly flammable with an open flame but can be processed to increase the surface area for use with a ferrocerium rod as well. An old Sami method of making fire is to roll tinder in a birch bark tube and then place an ember in the back of this tube closest to the mouth and gently blow. This protects the ember while allowing heat to rise through the tinder and the birch bark. It also adds fuel for longevity once the fire is ignited.

TIPS AND TRICKS

1. Remember that the bow and drill is a machine; the longer the bow, the fewer strokes it takes to achieve revolutions of the spindle, and the smaller the spindle, the more revolutions per stroke of the bow. There is a happy medium that takes some experience to find. Much is dependent on your

own method and body type, but a good standard is to start with a thumb-sized spindle and 3' bow.

2. Always keep an eye out for rocks that may be hard enough to drive a spark from high-carbon tools. Pick up rocks as you are walking and try them. If they work, throw them in your pack; if not, toss them aside. Chert and flint will have a slick shine to it when wet and may be white, gray, or pale hues of red and pink; quartz will always be a good bet.

3. Collect tinder sources at any opportunity, even if just walking from one location to another. Keep an eye out for any hanging, stringy bark materials. Honeysuckle vines will shed thin layers of bark all year long.

4. Dead plants, especially goldenrod, have flammable flower tops and hollow stems. These are terrific sources of tinder and kindling and generally grow in large groves of open fields.

5. A small stub from a used candle is always a good safety device to have when fire starting. Light the candle with the first open flame and set it aside until the fire has become sustainable. If you need a longer open flame for marginal materials, this will save precious lighter fluid. Candles are much easier to make than a new lighter.

— Chapter 5 —
SHELTERING

"Shelter provides a microenvironment that supplements inadequate clothing or allows you to shed cumbersome layers, especially when you want to stop moving or when you want to sleep in cold weather. Shelter also enhances the effect of a warming fire."

—Mors Kochanski

When planning for shelter you need to consider both long-term and short-term options. Even if you intend to build a base camp with a permanent shelter, you might still need to travel for a night or two to hunt, trap, or fish. For this reason, your kit should include a system that takes you easily from cabin to woods with supplies that will be useful in either situation. The base of this kit will include:

- Waterproof tarp (Egyptian cotton oilcloth works well here)
- Wool blanket
- Simple sleeve of canvas (like a painter's canvas) if you plan to make a raised bed

THE FOUR Ws

As discussed in detail in *Bushcraft 101*, there are four critical elements to consider when looking for a place to build your shelter:

- Wind
- Water
- Wood
- Widowmakers

WIND

The direction of the wind will have an impact on your ability to safely keep a fire going and heat your shelter. Look for middle high-ground areas where the wind is present but not too strong.

WATER

Look for a nearby area such as a creek bed that can provide a steady source of water.

WOOD

You will need a lot of wood for the fire, building shelter, and making other resources. A large fallen tree provides a good source of firewood, and trees such as pines can provide a steady supply of fatwood.

WIDOWMAKERS

Examine the trees around you—especially large trees—very carefully for any dead branches that could pose a danger to you and your campsite.

ESTABLISHING A BASE CAMP

Setting up a **base camp** saves you from having to carry all of your supplies on your back at all times. Of course, building a more permanent shelter is a large undertaking, and it will likely take a couple days of work, maybe even as long as a week if you are without a helping hand. Bearing that in mind, the first thing you will need to do when you arrive at the place where you intend to construct your base camp is to build a temporary shelter to keep you until the permanent shelter is ready. Just remember that you need to finish building your permanent shelter before the weather demands one.

For your permanent shelter, you can either build a larger version of your temporary base camp (like a hunter's station) from natural materials, or you can pack a larger canvas shelter in your kit. Whichever you choose, it must have at least three sides for protection from inclement weather and a large fire backing or portable wood stove that is at least as high as the pitch or roof of the shelter. In colder weather a raised bed is a must, but if the weather is fair, a hammock may be enough. Following are tarp configurations that can be used for a roving-type camp, working-camp structures, and finally methods for building a permanent shelter.

ROVING CAMPS

In *Bushcraft 101* we discussed the most common tarp setups. Here you will learn about some simple makeshift camp convenience items that will make common tarp and other temporary setups even more comfortable.

TENTS

There are many types of canvas tents and yurts that can be easily transported as long as you have conveyances.

Remember that large canvases can be difficult to heat, so for a seasonal shelter, think about selecting something small. Much of the decision about what type of canvas shelter to use will depend on your environment. **Open-faced tents** like the Whelen provide three sides of coverage and can be used with a hammock. For colder weather I would recommend something that can house a stove like a small wall tent.

Small wall tents can be very comfortable and offer great protection from the elements especially if a stove jack is installed. Many of the gold rush miners lived in wall tents that were placed on raised platforms. These temporary structures were large enough that they could even hold a few small furnishings such as a chair and a small table. Within the wall tent you can easily fit a hammock, a cot, or even build a raised bed. The biggest convenience of the wall tent is that it provides coverage on all four sides, which makes it operate like a canvas cabin. An 8' × 10' wall tent provides plenty of room for one person. It can be used temporarily with all the same fixtures and amenities, such as lighting and sleep setups, that you will eventually use for a more permanent shelter.

STAKING AND TIE-OUT METHODS
No matter what kind of temporary shelter you use, it will need to be tied down or staked so that it stays secure. There are many methods for securing your shelter, all of which depend on the materials that were used to manufacture it and the environmental conditions in which it has been erected. I recommend staying away from grommets altogether; they seem to be the weakest link in any shelter no matter the material because they tend to weaken the surrounding fabric. Instead, opt for the tie-out or stake loops whenever possible. If you have only a blank canvas with no way to tie it off, place a toggle on the corners and fold it over the toggle; trap this with a jam knot on the corner of the tarp.

A toggle can be used to tie down a tent

You can also use a stone or even a wad of dead leaves to place a ball of sorts in the area that needs to be tied and then tie a jam knot over the whole thing. In the old days, musket balls were often used for this type of configuration.

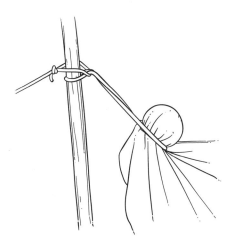

A ball tie-down on a tarp configuration

All tie lines should be made adjustable for tension so they can be tightened or loosened when necessary. Adding this adjustability makes it easy to set up and take down your shelter. To do this, use flat slabs of wood with a hole drilled on each end that is large enough for the ropes to pass through. The rope is then placed in this toggle, one end in each hole, and knotted. If you are using loops for tie-out points, it makes sense to pass the rope through the loop before knotting on one end of this sliding toggle. After this it can be looped over a stake and then adjusted for tension. Another way of doing this is to use a standard trucker's hitch knot with a tensioning loop on the tie-out ropes. You can also use a barrel knot, which will self-tighten when pressure is applied.

Another option is to stake your shelter right into the ground. In this way you are almost creating a microclimate, and wind and weather will have very little effect on it. A noisy, loose tarp that is blowing around in the wind will be an all-night aggravation. Be sure all lines are tight and secure enough to withstand any unexpected weather conditions. Stakes made of wood work well for longer-term camps because the wood swells with moisture, which further secures it into the ground. The length of the stake is really dependent on ground condition: Use longer stakes for moist ground and shorter stakes for dry ground.

If the ground is extremely hard, you might need to use metal instead. In those cases I recommend fashioning stakes from a ⅜" steel stock like rebar with a 2" × 120° bend at the top. If stakes are not practical at all, you can improvise with things like logs, rocks, or bags filled with something heavy like smaller rocks or dirt. If the ground is extremely soft, it may take a chain of two stakes to secure the tent in high wind conditions.

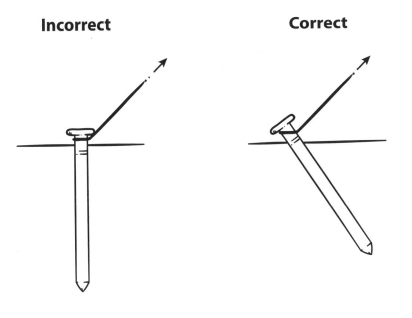

Incorrect　　　　　　　　**Correct**

Stake-driving angles

PERMANENT SHELTER OPTIONS

The best type of permanent shelter depends on the environment, seasonal changes, resources available, equipment on hand, and the skill level of the user. Here we will discuss a few simple designs that do not require vocational expertise. In my experience, anything that is too difficult or complicated to construct is likely to be left undone.

CAVES AND ROCK HOUSES

Long before man started constructing his own shelter he adopted existing elements in nature to be his home, just as animals do. These caves and stone shelters endure in nature, and although it takes a little effort to make them comfortable, they can still be a great choice if the situation arises. In fact, there are millions of people worldwide who live in cave dwellings.

THE DOWNSIDE OF CAVES

It is important to remember the dangers that may present themselves in natural dwellings.

A wet cave can be a miserable place to sleep. If you are in an area with high humidity or lots of annual rainfall, caves are not the best choice. Cave moisture creates several dangers, including bacteria growth, mold, weak stone integrity of the cave itself, and a dampness that could leave you cold most of the time. A cave might also already be home to insects and other mammals such as bats, cats, or bears.

> **BUSHCRAFT TIP**
>
> If you are considering using a cave as a permanent shelter dwelling, inspect it for signs of animals that may have set up housekeeping. Look for feces, bones, and smells of urine. Falling rock can also present a danger, so make a visual inspection with a good light source of the ceiling and walls. Look for fissures or cracks in the stone that might be compounded by heat from a fire. Consider the height of the ceiling. The lower the ceiling height of the cave, the more a fire will affect the structure's integrity. Caves with higher ceilings will also provide much better ventilation.

RAISED PLATFORM SHELTERS

A raised platform shelter can be constructed by attaching wood pieces with simple lashings and cross members to create the platform. Just remember that the more complex the shelter, the more resources and tools that are required to construct it. The raised platform should be at least 3'–5' above ground level; again, this depends on the factors like wildlife, resources, and environment. Make this platform at least 2' wider than the inside dimension of the shelter you plan to place on top of it and at least 6' longer to leave room for open work areas. The covering or construction of the shelter itself can be a simple hoop design or a square structure. The hoop design is by far the easiest to build and maintain, and it will shed water the best as well.

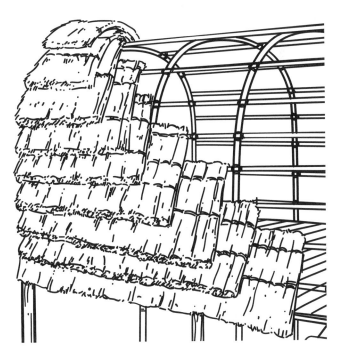

Hoop design on a shelter configuration

LOG CABINS
Building a small cabin with a single pitched roof is a fairly simple undertaking from a design perspective. However, it is labor-intensive and requires a great deal of timber resources. An

8' × 10' cabin should be sufficient for a single person. Anything larger will be difficult to heat. You will want logs of at least 8"–10" diameter for this, and size will dictate the number needed.

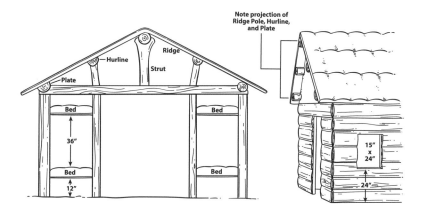

Basic log cabin design

EARTHEN STRUCTURES

Shelters constructed from earthen materials are a good option if the resources are available. Partial wood construction shelters can also be covered with earthen materials for far better insulation in cold-weather environments.

SOD

Sod is slabs of ground materials and dirt to which the existing plants or grasses are still attached. Sod makes good shelter coverage because it should continue growing foliage over time, which will only add to its waterproofing and insulation capabilities. Sod can be cut to any width and length but should always be at least 4" thick. If you intend to use sod materials on a roof, ensure that the supporting structure can hold the weight before covering. You will want semiclear sod that does not contain small trees or bushes, which may later grow large roots that interfere with the rest of the structure.

NATURAL CEMENTS

Natural cement has been used for thousands of years to build many things from shelter structures to hearths, ovens, and storage areas. You can even use natural cement to develop your own blocks or bricks.

The following materials are required to make natural cement:

- Clay-based soil (if the soil feels smooth and slick when wet, it most likely has a higher clay content)
- Grasses and longer fibers that can be used as rebar
- A source of water
- A bucket or container for mixing

To make the cement, collect enough clay-based soil to fill your bucket. You will also need a good armload of dry grasses about 6"–12" long or other fibrous plant materials. Long, dry grasses work much better than green grass for this project.

Now mix some water with the clay until you get a squishy consistency that is not too runny. If you are using this for a mortar or chink, mix it thinner. You can mix the cement right in the bucket, but I find that a tarp works very well for this process. Spread out the tarp, lay down the grasses first, and then dump the mud on top of them. The most effective way to incorporate the mix is with your bare feet so that the materials really grind together. You can fold the tarp over the materials and walk on the enclosed mass, or you can simply use your hands to make sure the grasses are well mixed and nothing is left dry or unmixed.

Use the cement immediately to create your structure or as mortar for your project. If you want to save it for later, you can shape it into bricks.

> **BUSHCRAFT TIP**
>
> To make bricks you can use the cement already created and shape it in a form made from wood. It will take several of these forms to make many bricks at a time. Pack the materials into the brick form and use another split stick as a scraper to level the top. Let the bricks dry in the sun for several days and they will shrink a little bit, making it very easy to remove them from the mold. You can also make fired bricks similar to the way you make clay pots, but the binder material used must be more selective, like cattail fluff or crushed shells.

CAMP AMENITIES

No matter the size or permanence of the base camp you decide to construct, there are a few camp amenities you should include for both comfort and convenience.

LIGHTING

You need to think about sources of lighting to use as the fire dies down or before the fire is built. Headlamps are fine for a quick outing as long as your kit includes spare batteries. For the long term, candles tend to work best. Besides providing light, candles also have an open flame to aid in emergency or late-night fire starting. Beeswax candles can also be melted and used for many other purposes such as a lubricant or wood polish. You can even rub it on your tools to prevent rusting.

A simple **lantern** can be fashioned from an empty can to protect the candle from going out in the wind. If your hunting or trapping campaign has been successful, use fat from the animal to make oil lamps. Any concave container, from a shell to a hollow piece of wood, will make an easy lamp. All you need is a wick, which can be made from any soluble material such as cotton rope or natural cordage. You can also use a ball of compressed cattail fluff or corded cedar bark for a quick, temporary wick.

Make **candles** by dipping a wick of natural cord into a pan of melted tallow, letting it cool, dipping again, and letting it cool. The thickness increases each time. The difference between tallow and lard is the tallow will harden at room temperature and lard will stay soft. Torches are easily made by dipping dead plant tops like mullein into fat and letting them dry.

SOAP

Many plants have natural **saponins**, chemicals that are created by the saponification process when making soaps. This substance occurs naturally in many plants and creates a nice lather that can be used as a natural soap. In the eastern woodlands, the best choice for this is the bracken fern because its root is high in saponins. Yucca is another American plant that can be used for this purpose.

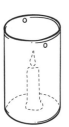

Melt end of candle to stick

Punch holes to let air in and light out

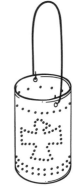

Coat hanger bale

Simple lantern made from a can

LATRINE

For short-term outings it is easy to simply walk away from camp and dig a small cat hole for a latrine. Outings that last more than a couple of days, however, will necessitate a pit latrine. This pit must be a comfortable distance from camp but well away from any groundwater source. Generally speaking, the **pit latrine** should be as deep as possible but should be kept to at least 3' above the water table. Finding a spot this far above the water table can be a tricky undertaking depending on camp location and elevation. If you find yourself needing to choose between a farther walk and possible groundwater pollution, do yourself a favor and take the walk up hill. A good practice for wilderness pit latrines is to add ashes from the campfire daily. This will cover the smell, break down the fecal matter, and detract pests like flies. Once the pit is full within a foot of the top, cover it with debris and dig a new pit in a different location. Consider this matter seriously at the outset when choosing a long-term camp location.

LINES

Ridge lines are the best place to hang a lantern, keep clothing off the ground, or suspend a bag of goodies that may be needed at night. Drying lines should always be used to ensure you have a place to air bedding material and clothing during the day or when wet. Beating a wool blanket hung over a line will keep it free of dirt, dead skin cells, and many pests.

ESTABLISHING A SLEEP SYSTEM

Sleeping gear can have a big impact on the weight of your supplies—a simple canvas and a couple of wool blankets can add as much as 20 pounds to your kit. Still, a good night's sleep of at least 6 hours is one of the most important aspects of long-term comfort and survival. Often my sleep system makes up two-thirds of my kit's weight. The following items are a solid basis for a sleep system that will be effective in either a temporary or permanent shelter:

- Wool blanket (or two)
- Materials for a raised bed
- Canvas
- Large needle, like a sail needle, that is heavy enough to puncture your canvas
- #36 bankline for stitching the canvas
- Synthetic sleeping bag in case you are not able to return to the base camp for a night or two

BUILDING A RAISED BED

A **raised bed** is the best weapon against ground temperature when sleeping. You can manufacture a simple mattress, or browse bed, with a heavy painter's canvas or wool blanket. First fold your canvas widthwise (not lengthwise). It is okay for your feet to hang off the end, but it is important that your bed be wide enough for you to roll over without falling. Thread your needle with the #36 bankline and whip-stitch the ends of your canvas together on two sides. The stitching does not have to be perfect; anything between 1"–2" stitches will work fine. It should not take more than about 15 minutes to stitch up two sides of the canvas.

Next stuff your bed with leaves and grass. This is the most time-consuming part of manufacturing a raised bed. Stuff the bed and then compress the material to make room for more. Stuff the bed again and compress the material to make room for more. This process can take as long as an hour. When the bed is packed with about 4" of compressed insulation, stitch up the last side with your whip stitch.

SETTING UP YOUR SLEEP AREA

Fold over your tarp and lay it down where it will act as a moisture barrier between the ground and your raised bed. The wool blanket will keep you warm while sleeping. Carry some sort of bag—even your haversack—that can be emptied at night and filled with spare clothing to act as a pillow. A pillow is a tremendous comfort that is often completely underrated.

HAMMOCKS

Hammocks are an option but will require an underquilt or some sort of insulation to battle convection issues that come with colder weather. A cheap way to deal with this issue is to place a thick pad like a ground mat in the hammock and a reflective batting on top of that. Then place your sleeping bag or blankets right on this pad. Reflectix is an insulation used for the home and can be purchased at any hardware store. It comes in 2'–3' widths and is basically a bubble wrap with Mylar covering. The other option is an underquilt that will trap warm air between the quilt and the hammock.

TIPS AND TRICKS

1. There are many good, modern synthetic materials you can use as a sleeping bag. Just remember that these materials will not be as long lasting over time and are much more susceptible to things such as an errant spark from an all-night fire.

2. Canvas that is untreated may be susceptible to mold. Treating it before use with a guarding agent is prudent. Canvas can also be very susceptible to UV breakdown at altitudes of about 3000', so treat it or buy Sunforger tent canvas, which will be the best bet for a long-lasting shelter.

3. Most red-meat animals have tallow in their fat, and most white-meat animals like hogs have lard.

4. In areas where stakes will not penetrate hard earth or rocks, long logs or large rocks can be used as substitutes for stakes.

5. Remember that any insulation made from natural material on the ground to battle conduction should be 4" thick when compressed.

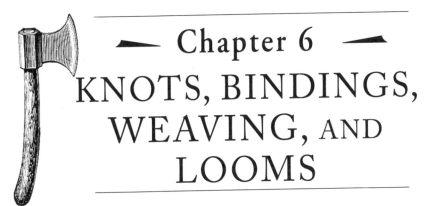

— Chapter 6 —
KNOTS, BINDINGS, WEAVING, AND LOOMS

"Bushcraft is what you carry in your mind and your muscles."
—RAY MEARS

Cordage is one of the most valuable resources that you carry in your kit. Its uses are endless, from lashing objects together in woodworking projects to weaving additional implements to add comfort to your camp.

CORDAGE AND ROPES

For long-term excursions, here are the most beneficial and multifunctional ropes and materials to carry in your kit:

1. Natural ropes
2. Paracord
3. Bankline
4. Natural strings
5. Webbing
6. Mule tape

NATURAL ROPE VERSUS SYNTHETIC ROPE

Natural rope is easier to use and far more versatile than most synthetics. This is true especially when it is broken down into smaller fibers or cords. Synthetic ropes, such as rigging rope or Kevlar climbing and static-line ropes, are widely available and can be a good resource to keep on hand if you have room in your kit. Just know that while these synthetics are strong for their relative size, the fibers tend to break down after lengthy exposure in the wilderness, which makes them difficult to use.

MAKING ROPE

Making rope is a useful skill to possess in the event you find yourself in a situation that requires more cordage than what you currently have in your kit. You can make a rope by combining and twisting three or more strands together. There are three components to a rope:

- **Fibers:** The fibers are the smallest materials that are twisted together to create the yarns.
- **Yarns:** Yarns are multiple fibers twisted together in the same direction.
- **Strands:** Strands are multiple yarns again twisted in a single direction.

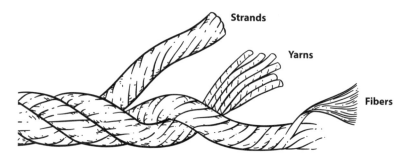

Rope components

OPERATING A ROPE TWISTER

Rope is made from multiple strands twisted in two different directions. It only takes one person to operate a simple rope twister, which can produce lengths of rope that are about 20' long. To make enough, you will need to feed about eleven times the amount of cord you intend to produce through the rope twister. Attach one end of the cord to a stationary object and make one loop so that you can attach it to the spinner and twist. Start by spinning in a clockwise fashion until the cord begins to wind on itself when it is slack. At this point, divide the cord in thirds and make two loops: one to place over the original stationary object and one to place around the twister. You should now have three strands of larger cord again between the twister and the static end. Begin spinning again in counterclockwise fashion until the desired tightness is achieved. Once the rope is finished, pull hard against the static object to "set" the rope. Cut the ends and whip-stitch them to finish your rope.

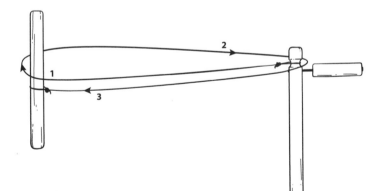

Step 1

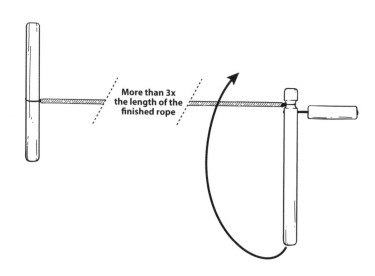

More than 3x
the length of the
finished rope

Step 2

CONSERVING CORDAGE

One of the most important skills in wilderness survival is **proper use of cordage**. Whether it is synthetic rope you have carried in your kit or natural rope you have manufactured yourself, cordage is a precious resource that should be treated with care. In fact, I prefer to use knots that can easily be untied so that the rope can always be recovered without having to cut it. When working with synthetic rope, I also avoid cutting lengths shorter than about 20', or four "pulls" from the roll, unless it is absolutely necessary. By "pulls" I mean pulls from the roll that are the length of my outstretched arms, from one hand to the other. For this reason, it is always best to use natural bark cordage for small binding or lashing projects.

KNOTS

Bushcraft 101 covered some basic knots (bowline, fisherman's, Prusik, timber hitch, clove hitch, and trucker's hitch) that you need to know when setting up a short-term camp. Understanding how to make joining and jamming knots and knowing when to use them will help you conserve cordage and ropes on a long-term excursion.

STOP KNOTS

The **stop** knot is used as a security knot in conjunction with jamming and joining knots. Both joining and jamming knots are used to join two cords or ropes together to increase cordage length. A stop knot is an overhand knot that is tied to keep the line from slipping under tension, passing back through a hole, or even slipping through another knot.

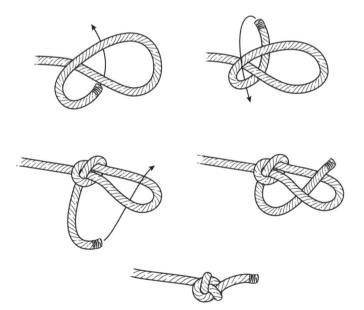

Stop knot

JOINING KNOTS

A **joining** knot is used to connect two different pieces of cord that may or may not be of the same diameter.

Sheet Bend

The sheet bend is a great knot for joining two ropes of equal diameter when loops are not available on the end of the lines.

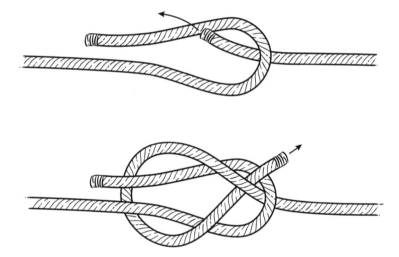

Sheet bend knot

Loop to Loop (Square Knot)

The loop to loop is generally useful when joining lines with loops on the end of both lines.

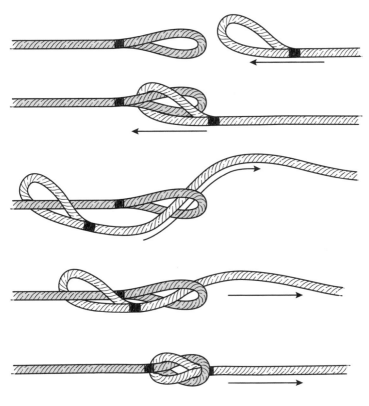

Loop to loop

JAMMING KNOTS

A **jamming** knot is used to join two pieces of cordage of the same diameter together, especially if the line to be extended has a loop on the end. The beauty of these knots is how easily they can be loosened for adjustment or removal on the fly or in a hurry.

Canadian Jam (Arbor Knot)

The Canadian jam is best used as a tensioning knot when cinching a load such as a blanket to a frame or a bedroll. This knot can also work for things like tensioning two cross braces on a raft.

Canadian jam

Lark's Head Jam

This knot works very well when attaching cords to a line for the purpose of weaving or hanging something from them. You can even use this type of knot for toggles when you are not able to double over the line or when you simply need to hang a single line. It is best used with a stop knot on the tag end.

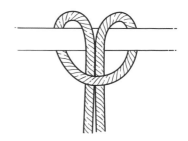

Lark's head jam

Clove Hitch Jam

The clove hitch jam is a knot that will actually cause a constriction to the attached line to keep the tails from sliding independently. Essentially this knot self-locks under tension.

IN-LINE LOOPS

In-line loops are for a static hold or connection but can also be used as a static pulley for tensioning around an object.

Slip Loop or Hitch Loop

The slip loop is used to make a tension device, kind of like a pulley. It is used for things like holding loads tight or pulling a ridgeline taut. The slip loop can be easily incorporated into the standing line and comes undone with a simple pull.

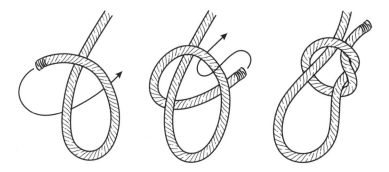

Slip loop

Butterfly Loop

The butterfly loop will form a stable and secure loop that does not slip within a line. This knot can be easily broken or untied even when it is under tension. You can also easily adjust the size of the loop.

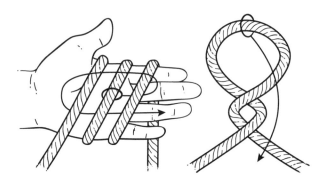

Butterfly loop

SLIDERS

Sliders are defined as knots that will slide up and down a static rope, tied on itself, or knots made by attaching one rope to another.

Barrel Knots/Blood Knots

Barrel knots can be used on one side of a standing or looped line to create a slider that can be adjusted for tensioning guy lines. If it is tied on two opposing lines, it becomes a joining or blood knot. The blood knot is often used for monofilament or fishing lines.

Barrel knot

END-OF-LINE LOOPS

These knots are simply used to create a loop tied in one end of a line or rope. This can be used as an attachment point or a tensioning loop around an object as when you are putting up a ridgeline around a tree.

Poacher's Noose

The poacher's noose is a specialty knot used for snaring that incorporates a lark's head loop on the end of the snare loop so that it will constrict and stay tight under tension.

Poacher's noose

Figure Eight

Figure-eight loops create end-of-line loops that are easily broken or untied after tension is applied to the loop. These loops work much better than a simple overhand knot to create end-of-line loops.

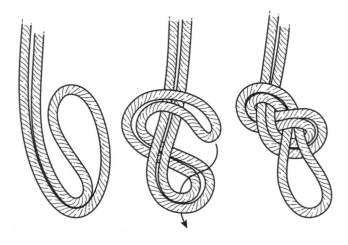

Figure eight

Bowline

The bowline is another end-of-line loop that has a few advantages over the others. For one, it tightens or constricts against the line as tension is applied, which makes it a good rescue loop. It can also easily be tied into the line after the rope is already passing around another object.

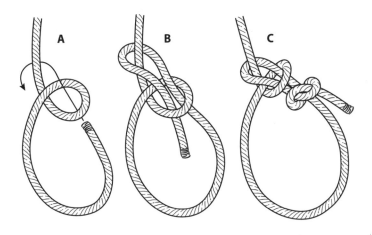

Bowline

HITCHES

Hitches are generally temporary connections that can be easily untied or adjusted.

Slippery Hitch

The slippery hitch is a quick hitch to secure objects that are not under a load. It could be used when hanging a cord from another line or a branch. It is a quick-release knot so it is especially helpful for things such as tying a line from a boat to a tree on the shore.

Slippery hitch

Trucker's Hitch

The trucker's hitch incorporates an in-line loop to secure a load or a tensioned line. It can be set up to quick-release so that loads can be easily untied or so that ridgelines at the campsite can be easily moved.

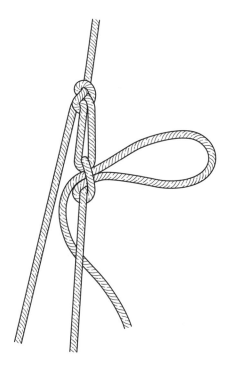

Trucker's hitch

Timber Hitch

The timber hitch is a great starting hitch for any lashings because it is a constricting knot that relies on friction in order to hold. It can be easily undone to recover cordage and can be used at the end of bowstrings.

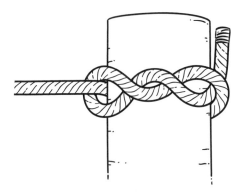

Timber hitch

BINDINGS

Bindings are a combination of wraps, knots, and hitches that are used for securing something. They can be used to secure loads that will be transported over a distance or to secure a series of contents rolled into a package such as a tarp or blanket. They can even be used to attach a bundle to something else such as a pack frame, horse, or sled.

BASKET WEAVING

Baskets make excellent containers for storage and carrying food while you harvest it. The simplest method of basket weaving starts with making a cross lashing in a square-lash fashion with four flexible twigs, shoots, or splits on each side for a total of eight sticks. You will need to add a ninth stick into this as you begin to weave your basket. You can weave in any material such as vines, bark, or splits. Weave in and out of the splits. You can start to shape this weave into a basket by gradually lifting the sides and controlling the tightness of the weave to form a round container. Finish this off by wrapping another piece of the material in an overhand running-stitch fashion around the top and trim any excess sticks or twigs off the finished product.

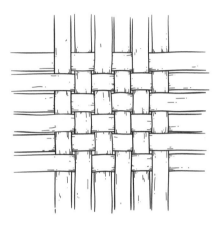

Basket weave

SIMPLE COIL BASKETRY

Coil basketry is a simple skill that employs pliable materials to make containers. It takes a good amount of cordage to sew a coil basket—especially a large one—but the materials used to make the coils are quite simple. Choose items that can be doubled in half without breaking, such as pine needles and other leaves. Then you will need some bankline and a shuttle or a needle. A large sail needle works very well here, but you can also make your own out of wood or bone. Start with a section of the material you plan to coil. Double it over and wrap it into a tube, and then make progressive coils in a circular fashion, wrapping or sewing with the bankline to hold them together.

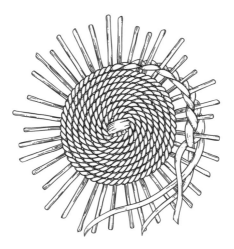

Coil basketry

BARK BASKETS

Bark harvested from the yellow poplar in the spring can be fashioned into a durable basket. Yellow poplar bark can also be manipulated into tubular shapes and used for quivers. To harvest the bark, score the outer bark of the tree down to the sapwood with a knife or axe. Then score another line in a circular fashion above and below that first line. This method, known as "ringing the tree," will usually kill the tree, so take care to select a poplar with a lot of other resources that you can use over time.

Once the bark is scored you can use a sharp stick or spud to peel it away from the tree. For a simple basket, cut a piece of bark that is two-and-a-half times longer than the finished basket needs to be high. Select a width based on the size you want your container to be when it is complete. Cut two half-moons on the outside of the bark right in the middle of your piece. The half-moons should be facing each other so that their bottom and top tips are touching. These cuts will be the fold lines that form the bottom of the basket. You can then fold up the sides and lace them. Fold up the piece with the bark facing out, and drill holes up the sides using your awl. You can use strong cordage to lace up the basket with simple x stitches. Add a handle to the top if needed. Yellow poplar is my favorite for this, but you can also use birch. If you plan to only make a very small container, maybe you can avoid stripping a large section of bark. In these cases, place a coating of mud over the open area of the tree to help protect it and give it a chance to heal.

WEAVING

Weaving is broad skill that can produce anything from straps for a backpack to baskets or even shelter coverings. It can be as simple as weaving together small strands of cordage or as complex as using a loom to weave threads into a wide textile. In this section I will describe some of the most versatile weaving techniques that have served me well in wilderness outings.

Before we get started, here are some terms you should know:

- **Crosshatch**—Two series of parallel lines that flow in opposite directions so that they cross each other.
- **Warp**—The set of lengthwise threads on a loom.
- **Weft**—The thread that is drawn through the warp threads to create a textile.
- **Shed**—The separation between the upper and lower warp threads through which the weft is woven.
- **Heddle**—The part of the loom that separates the warp threads so that the weft can be threaded through them.
- **Shuttle**—Anything that will carry the weft across the warp and through the shed.

DIAGONAL FINGER WEAVING

Diagonal finger weaving is an effective technique to make short straps that can be used for things such as backpacks, gun slings, or other projects that are not particularly long or wide.

To get started, place two nails about 6" apart in a piece of stationary wood such as a workbench. Your weaving stick will rest on top of these nails while you work. Select a weaving stick about ½" in diameter and 12"–16" long. Double 5 strands of cord, such as jute string, over the weaving stick and secure each cord with a lark's head knot. You will then have 10 strands hanging off your weaving stick.

Use a second stick, similar in diameter and length to your weaving stick, as a **winding stick** to be placed below the two nails that are holding your weaving stick. Wrap finished product around the winding stick as you weave. This allows you to stay close to your work area and use the tension created as the weaving stick rolls against those nails to create a secure weave.

Now it is time to get started. Set your weaving stick on top of the nails. Loop the tenth strand over the right-hand nail in your workbench. For the first row, take the first strand, which will be your active strand, and loop it under the second strand, over the third strand, under the fourth strand, over the fifth . . . and so forth until you reach the ninth strand. Then take the tenth strand off the nail and replace it with your active strand.

For the second row, take what is now your first strand and loop it, this time over the second strand, under the third strand, over the fourth strand . . . and so forth until you reach the ninth strand. Pull the tenth strand off the nail and replace it with your active strand.

Continue this process, taking the first strand in the line and alternating the under/over weave and then switching that pattern in the next row to the opposite, until your piece reaches the desired length. At this time, take your tenth strand and fashion it into a clove hitch to finish the strap.

CROSS WEAVING

Cross weaving is a process that can be used with any textured material like barks or cattail leaves. Cross weaving involves hatching and can be used to make materials as large or as small as you need. It can also be shaped into almost any configuration needed. Picture a tic-tac-toe board in which the lines of the board alternate over and under each other to form a weave.

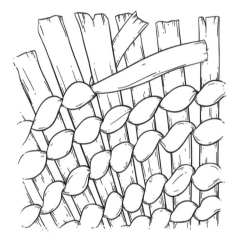

Cross weaving

WOODLAND LOOM

You can manufacture a large-scale **woodland loom** as a means for creating big sleeping mats or covering for shelters like wigwams. To make a woodland loom, secure one long sapling about waist high on a tree in a T fashion with a simple lashing. Place several stakes in the ground away from but directly in front of this crossbar. These stakes are your looming poles and should be lined up parallel to the tree. The longer the project, the farther the stakes should be placed. The width of your project will be determined by the number of stakes in the row. Then create another bar from a similar-sized sapling as the one you used for the T. You now have the components of your loom. You will then alternate the warps for the weave with strong cordage. Alternate so that the first warp is fixed to the sapling you secured to the tree. The next warp is secured to a stake. The next warp is secured to the sapling on the tree. The one after that is secured to the next stake in the line. Continue setting up the warps in this pattern until you reach the final stake. Use the crossbar as your heddle. Once the warps are complete you will be able to raise and lower the heddle to place wefts of material in the loom, alternating over and under them. Use another sapling as a beater stick to tighten the wefts as you go. This operation works best with more than one person.

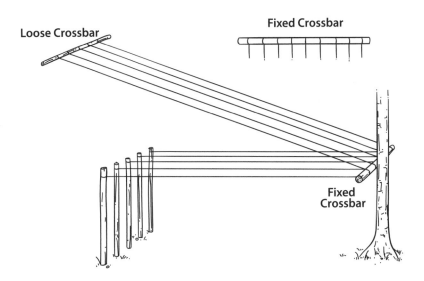

Woodland loom

TABLET WEAVING

Tablet weaving, like diagonal finger weaving, is used to make straps that are strong but not too wide. In tablet weaving, however, you will not be manipulating the individual components of your project as much because you will not be using your fingers. In tablet weaving, cards, or flat pieces into which holes have been drilled, operate as the shed.

To begin, you will need to create an even number of square cards that are about 3¼" on all sides. For this you can use wood, cardboard, plastic, or any other material that is fairly stiff. Drill 4 holes, one in each corner, in each of your cards. These cards will act as the heddle, and one thread will pass through each of the holes to create the warps. So if you have 12 cards, you will have 48 warps.

The loom can be any two points such as sticks, for example, to which you can attach your threads. When you begin weaving, you can either hold the end of the loom that is nearest to the cards or attach it to your belt. The far end can be secured by a slipknot to a stationary object like a tree. Once you determine the number of warps, it is time to cut your string. Take the number of warps and cut half that many strings. If you want 48 warps, cut 24 strings. Fold each string in half and secure to the near end of your loom with a lark's head knot. Once all the strings are attached, you can now thread each through the holes in your cards.

Once the warps are established you will need a shuttle to pass the weft through them. A net needle will work perfectly, or any needle that has an eye big enough to hold your cordage. To begin weaving, pass the shuttle through the shed, which is the gap between the top holes in your cards and the bottom holes. Once you reach the end of the line, turn your cards a quarter turn clockwise. Now pass the weft through the shed once more and, once you reach the end of the line, turn your cards another quarter turn clockwise. Repeat these steps until you reach the desired length. To finish the piece, simply tie off and braid the remaining length of strands.

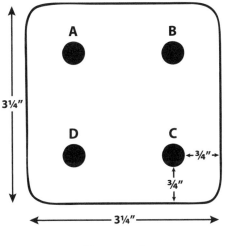

Tablet weaving

A SIMPLE PEG LOOM

Simple **peg looms** are useful because they can be adjusted to work with materials of all sizes to make products of all dimensions. For the sake of our instructions, assume we are using wool yarn to make a scarf. When weaving with a peg loom, the string threaded through each peg is the warp. The yarn wrapped around each peg is the weft.

CONSTRUCTING A PEG LOOM

To build a peg loom you will need the following materials:

- 1 piece of wood: 2" × 4" and about 1'–2' long
- 8 dowel rods about 1" × 6"–8"
- A drill

Drill a series of holes into your 2" × 4" into which each of your dowel rods will sit. These rods are your pegs for the loom. Drill a hole at the base of each peg through which you will thread the warp strings. These holes should be high enough that when the pegs are placed in the holes on the 2" × 4" you can see them above the edge.

SETTING UP THE PEG LOOM

Determine how long you want your final product to be and use double the amount of cordage. Now thread one piece of yarn through each peg. I use a small wire hook to help pull the string though the peg holes. Pull the yarn through until both sides of the yarn hang evenly from the peg hole. These hanging yarns will operate as the warp.

Now that your peg loom is set up, it is time to begin weaving. Pull the tail from your ball of yarn (or whatever material you are using) and tie it to your first peg. Use an overhand knot that is secure and will not come undone. Pass the yarn behind the second peg, in front of the third peg, behind the fourth peg, in front of the fifth peg, behind the sixth peg. Now bring your yarn back to the first peg by passing it in front of the sixth peg, behind the fifth peg, in front of the fourth peg, behind the third peg, in front of the second peg, and in front of your first peg. Now send that yarn back down the line of pegs. Each row of wraps you make around the pegs will essentially lock in the previous row of wraps because they will wind in the opposite direction.

Continue passing the weft around the pegs until your stacks of wraps are about three-quarters of the way up your pegs. As you weave, push down the rows of wraps with a beater stick or your hands. This not only tightens up the rows on your work but also allows you to fit more rows on the pegs.

BUSHCRAFT TIP

You can expand your peg loom so that it will work with projects and materials of all sizes. Simply drill an additional series of peg holes above and below your first row. The holes can be farther apart for wider materials or closer together for smaller cordage. Make the holes bigger for bigger pegs or smaller. The larger setting in your peg loom can be used for shreds of animal hides. Peg looms can have as many as 30–40 pegs, depending on the width of your materials and desired size of your finished product. You can place such large looms on sawhorses for stability.

I like to tie a slipknot in the bottom of my hanging yarns to make sure that my weaving holds together as I unload the pegs. Pull the pegs out of their holes and slip each stack of wraps off the pegs and slide them onto your hanging yarns. Put the pegs back into the holes and wrap the yarn around them again, alternating directions, until they reach about halfway or three-quarters of the way up the pegs. Once more, slip them off the pegs and slide them onto your weft. Continue doing this until the piece reaches your desired length.

INKLE LOOM

An **inkle loom** is a tape loom that can be used to make narrow pieces such as belts, trim for clothing, haversack straps, and sashes. Constructing the inkle loom is challenging, but once set up and threaded, weaving on the loom is very straightforward and simple.

CONSTRUCTING AN INKLE LOOM

To make an inkle loom you will need the following materials:

- 1 (30" × 1" × 4") piece of wood
- 3 (15" long) pieces of 1" × 4" wood
- 1 piece of scrap wood 15"–20" long

- 1 piece of dowel rod about 32" long
- Wood glue
- Wood screws: 4 (1"), 8 (2")
- Drill with a #2 Phillips bit
- Saw

Lay the 30" piece of wood down on your workspace. Spread some wood glue on the flat end of your first 15" piece and place it at 15°–20° angle on the right flat end of the 30" board. Secure the wood by drilling in a couple of wood screws. Take the second 15" board and place it about a foot away from the first on the 30" piece, at the same slight angle in the opposite direction. Secure with wood glue and a couple of screws. Attach the scrap wood at the bottom edge of your 30" piece, perpendicular to the 15" pieces. This scrap will act as the base to the inkle loom.

Next saw your dowel rod into pegs that are equal lengths of 6". You will need 8 pegs for the inkle loom. Drill a ½"-deep hole in the bottom of each peg (I use a vise to hold the peg steady while drilling) and attach 3 of them to the flat side of each angled 15" piece of wood. The first peg on each piece of 15" wood should be attached 2" from the top, the second 2" from the bottom, and the third right in the middle—about 8" from the bottom. To attach, put a little wood glue on the back of each peg and also on the screw threads themselves for extra security. Attach the seventh peg to the front end of the 30" piece of wood just under the lowest peg on the first angled 15" board.

Attach the last peg to the front of the third piece of 15" wood. Use a C-clamp to secure this piece of wood to the 30" board on the loom while you thread the pegs. You can remove the C-clamp once the pegs are threaded and tension is established between the loom and the eighth peg. This piece of wood will move back and forth as you begin operating the loom.

THREADING THE INKLE LOOM

You will need two sets of cordage to weave on your inkle loom. I generally use a jute string and often two different colors, one for the warps and another for the weft, which produces an attractive pattern. Tie the tail of your first set of cordage to the 15" board that holds peg 8. Now bring your string over the top of pegs 1 and 2, under peg 3, over peg 4, under peg 5, over peg 6, skip the heddle peg (7), and under peg 8. Now bring your string back to the top of the loom, but this time go under peg 1 and then again over 2, under 3, over 4, under 5, over 6, skip 7, and under 8. Bring the string to the top of the loom once more but this time string it over 1, over 2 . . . and so forth. Essentially you will be alternating your over/under for only peg 1. The direction of string for the other pegs will always remain the same. Continue to place the warps this way until you reach your desired project width. This space between the strings that were passed over peg 1 and those that were passed under peg 1 will create your shed, and your shuttle will pass through this space.

A **net needle** works very well as a shuttle for the inkle loom. To begin weaving, attach your second supply of string to the warp strings in front of peg 8. Load your shuttle with the string. Attach with a simple clove hitch so you can easily undo the knot later. For the first row, push the warp strings in front of peg 1 down to make the shed. Pass your shuttle through this space. For the second row, push the warp strings in front of peg 1 up, and pass your shuttle through this space. As you continue with this pattern, use your beater stick to push down each weft on the warps as you loom.

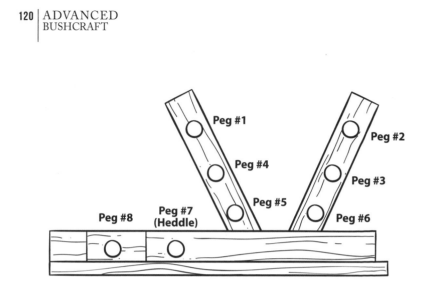

Inkle loom

ROTATING THE PIECE

After you have been weaving for a while and the weft is about an inch away from the heddle, it is time to rotate your piece. Undo the clove hitch that you used to attach the weft to the loom and tie it around the warp strings, securing it with a tight overhand knot. Now that your second cordage is free from the loom, pull the work away from you so that it is moving backward over the base of the loom and push the heddle strings up. Keep pulling the work backward and pushing the heddle strings up until the woven piece is winding under the loom and the warp in front of you is clear and ready to receive the weft.

WAIST LOOMS

Waist looms are one of the easiest ways to create long pieces of strapping such as tumplines if you do not have a full-sized inkle loom at your disposal. What makes the waist loom an appealing option is that you can weave projects of unlimited length. The weaver uses himself as the base of the loom with a stick and a waist strap or two metal rings. The warps are separated by a warp loop, and then the heddle strings are attached to a floating stick. The warps can then be manipulated by lifting the warp or heddle string to open a shed. The weft is woven into the shed with a shuttle of your choosing. Use another stick to roll up the completed product as the weaving progresses.

NETS AND NET MAKING

If you plan to spend time in an area with waterways, **net making** will prove to be one of the most valuable skills you will ever learn. You can make nets of any shape, size, or dimension to fit your needs. A good gill net (or stop net, as they are sometimes called) is a reliable source of food. Nets are wonderful to have on hand because they can also be multipurposed to cover and haul cargo or incorporated in land traps when capturing live food.

GILL NETS
Building a gill net takes a little effort but is an invaluable skill for long-term sustainability in the wilderness. These nets can be placed in a creek to catch fish or small mammals. For net building you will need the following:

- Large quantity of cordage with a thin diameter (I prefer #6 bankline)
- Small amount of a thick cordage (like #36 bankline)
- Net needle (these can be handmade with pine or cedar but commercial versions are also available in plastic)
- Mesh gauge that is the same width as your net needle

LOADING THE NET NEEDLE

First tie a clove hitch into your thin cordage and slip it over the point in your net needle. Flip the net needle to the back, bring the cordage down to the end of the net needle, wrap it around the base, bring it back up and wrap it around the point again, flip the net needle to the front, wrap the cordage around the base, back up around the center point, flip the needle to the back, and so forth until your cordage is loaded about three-quarters of the way up the point in your net needle.

SETTING UP THE MESH

Tie your head line to two stationary objects so that it stretches out at a height that is comfortable for you to begin working. This thicker cordage will act as your head line, and you will build your mesh by attaching the cordage from the net needle directly to this line.

Pull line from the point of the net needle and attach it to the head line with a clove hitch. You are now ready to secure your thin cordage to your head line with a series of knots. Using a mesh gauge ensures that every space in your mesh is the same width. Remember, the size of the spaces in your mesh determine what you will catch. If your spaces are 2" wide, anything that is smaller than 2" will be able to escape.

Bring your net needle line up at an angle and wrap it behind and over the head line and mesh gauge. Now bring the net needle line up again, but this time wrap it behind and over only the head line and make a knot around the loop you just made. Move like this, over the mesh gauge and head line, and then over just the head line and around your loop, until you have 15 knots in your head line.

OPERATING THE NET NEEDLE

Now that the cord from your net needle is secured to the bankline you will start forming the mesh. Begin where your needle is positioned at the right-hand side of your knots and work your way back to the first clove hitch. Hold your mesh gauge below the 15 loops you created with your first set of knots. Bring your net needle cord behind the mesh gauge and through the first loop. Pull the line the whole way through and tighten it against that mesh gauge. Then bring your line back up and around the back of your loop to make a knot. Work this way through all the loops until you get back to your first clove hitch. Hold the mesh gauge against your second set of loops and work your way to the end of the line, continuing to add to the loops until you reach your desired length.

FUNNEL NETS

Funnel nets are designed to be placed with the opening on the upstream side of the stream. They can then be pegged in place, and you can create a further funnel with natural debris or bait them for larger animals like turtles. A funnel net is constructed like a gill net, except for the head rope. Here, circle and lash a natural material like a green branch as a hoop at the head of your funnel. You can add additional hoops to the inside after the net is completed if you are working with a very long product. In this trap the fish will swim in but cannot turn around in the back of the funnel.

TUMPLINES

Tumplines, sometimes called **burden straps**, have been used for hundreds of years. Many cultures to this day still use a tumpline so that people can carry heavy loads on their backs, burdens that may be too large or cumbersome for normal pack straps. The tumpline is a strap that extends around the load itself and is worn on the crown of the head. The wearer slightly bends at the waist so that the weight is actually carried down the spine of the back and no tension is placed on the neck or shoulder muscles. Tumplines can be made from cordage, rope, or strapping and are sometimes hand woven and ornately decorated. Most measure about 6'–12' in length and have an approximate 2' area in the center that is wider than the rest of the strap. Some even have decorative split tails at the end that hang for 2'–3'.

TIPS AND TRICKS

1. Reverse-wrap, two-ply cordage can be made from an existing material such as a bankline to increase tensile strength or with natural fibers like barks twisted together.
2. A fisherman's knot is the best for joining any cordage in a netting or weaving project.
3. A separate tool, called a beater stick, can be made to essentially pack the wefts while weaving and will increase the durability and overall quality of the finished product.
4. If you plan to carve tools like needles and shuttles from natural materials, it pays to use dry woods as a green wood will usually crack when carved thin.

— Chapter 7 —

TRAPPING

"There is but one way to learn to do a thing and that is to do it."
—Daniel Carter Beard, *The Field and Forest Handy Book*

The topic of primitive trapping could fill an entire volume of its own, but I will cover just the most important information you need to become an effective, self-reliant trapper. In the old days, trappers used a combination of steel and primitive traps that were built using readily available materials. This would ensure good numbers of fur were taken without having to carry a hundred or more traps to the line. In an extended wilderness stay it is absolutely necessary to carry steel traps, but you must also have a direct knowledge of what it takes to successfully use primitive trapping methods. Metal traps did not become popular until the mid-1700s. Before then, many animals were caught using methods taught in the forests of Europe and in the United States by Native American mentors. When considering trapping as a means for survival, you are less concerned with specific species that provide fur and are instead focused on looking for edible meat sources. In order to be successful a trapper you need to first understand the progression of lower-food-chain resources (which animals other animals eat) to larger, more trap-worthy animals. You need to be clear about which animal you are hunting and how to identify signs of that animal when setting your traps. You should have a good working knowledge of traps for three main food sources: mammals, fish, and fowl.

ANIMAL BEHAVIOR

Effective trapping requires some basic knowledge of animal behavioral patterns. You need to understand:

- What they eat
- Where they live
- Where they travel

Animals are predictable. They need the same things we do: a comfortable place to sleep, water, and food. Outside of satisfying basic needs, their sole purpose in life is reproduction of their species. Animals are most relaxed when sleeping, followed by traveling to and from a feeding or watering area. They are most wary and cautious when actually feeding or watering. Travel routes are excellent places to set traps because animals are opportunistic in nature and can often be lured with bait. Remember that animals usually travel the same routes, and this makes it easy to learn their patterns. Their tendency to operate in patterns also makes it easy for them to recognize when something has changed in their direct environment. While scent or human odor is nothing new to an animal, a change such as a trap set in the area may take a couple of passes before it overwhelms their curiosity. Be prepared to wait it out and try not to get anxious when a trap has not been visited or tampered with 48–72 hours after being set.

An animal's diet is another important factor in trapping because a baited trap is a hundred times more likely to catch an animal than a curiosity-type set that is not baited. Snares in trails can be effective but present some challenges that will be covered later.

ANIMAL SIGN

Animal **sign** is the key to eliminating guesswork when setting your traps. Only trap where there is sign. Sign is anything the animal leaves as a trace that indicates it may have passed through the area. There are seven types of sign you need to know that will help you identify things like species, eating habits, and population numbers:

1. **Tracks:** Examining tracks is the easiest way to identify the species. This can also help determine population numbers, frequency of travel in that area, and even preferred food in cases where you can tell that one animal has been trailing another.

2. **Scat:** Scat left when an animal defecates can also help you identify species as well as what food source the animal is currently foraging.

3. **Slough:** Slough is something from the animal's body left behind after it is gone. Examples include a strand of hair on a fence wire, a feather dropped while preening, or shed snakeskin.

4. **Remains:** The dead body of an animal will not only provide possible resources such as bait and attractants for other traps, but it also may give some idea of what other animals are in the area.

5. **Refuse:** Refuse is the animal's garbage, which will help identify its species and its travel routes. For instance, a squirrel **midden,** or refuse heap, is its favorite spot and will be

littered with shells from the nuts it has been eating. A beaver or muskrat leaves behind chewed trees and branches.

6. **Dens**: A den is an animal's home. It can be a hole in the ground, in a bank, or in the hollow of a tree. The type of den is often a sure indicator of the species. You can usually set traps at the entrance or exit.

7. **Odor**: Odor is the trickiest sign to detect, but cat urine has a distinct smell, as does rotten meat from a carnivore den where a fox might live. Obviously you'll smell a skunk in the area, but other subtle smells can be identified as well.

LOWER-FOOD-CHAIN RESOURCES

Animals at the lower end of the food chain are what every other animal seeks for food. Around the water's edge this group includes frogs, crayfish, fish, as well as mussels and snails. Seeking these food items for yourself and then delegating a portion of them to the traps you build will enable you to catch more sizable prey items. If you are in an area that contains no water sources, you will need to microtrap in order to secure animals you can use as bait: for instance mice, rats, and chipmunks. You can also choose to combine these techniques. Some of these resources, like larger fish and turtles, are full meals in themselves.

WATER-TYPE TRAPS

Net making is a difficult skill that can take a long time to master, but there are some nets that are easy to fashion and work well. Remember that any net will only catch prey that cannot exit the holes you have created, so many nets must be tailored to the intended fish or animal.

DIP NETS

Dip nets are usually attached to a hooped pole with which you can reach into the water and lift the target out while it is trapped. This pole can be fashioned from a green fork that is wrapped against itself to form the loop. The net is attached directly to this hoop while the tool is manufactured.

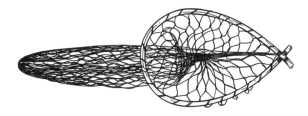

Dip net

GILL OR STOP NETS

Gill nets must be long enough to stretch from one side of a creek or small river to the other and deep enough to stretch from the top of the water to the bottom. This type of net is usually weighted with stones at the bottom and has some type of flotation device at the top.

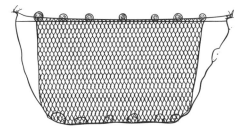

Gill net

You can drive fish into a gill net by walking downstream and chasing them into it. When they try to leave the net, their gills pass through the holes but their bodies cannot. You can see why it is critical to know the average size of the fish you are hunting in order to make an effective net.

SEINE NETS

A **seine net** is large with very small holes. It can be walked through a deeper water source and often has a long stick on each end that can be used to manipulate smaller fish to a place at the edge of the water where you can grab it.

FUNNEL NETS

Funnel nets resemble dip nets in many ways and can be made with a small diameter and elongated for fish-type traps, or they can be made with a large diameter and laid flat to trap animals when the net is lifted.

Funnel net

FENCES

Fences are used to guide fish to a certain location in the water or animals such as turtles to a location on the water's edge. They can be built from any natural material including stones, sticks, or even logs. Fencing called a **weir** can be used to trap fish in a smaller area where they can be hunted with a bow or gig.

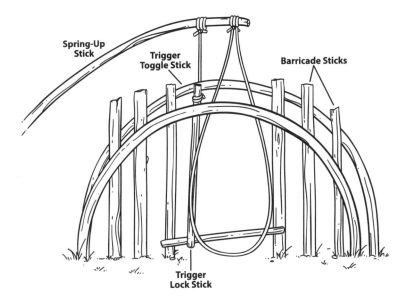

Fencing

FUNNELS

Funnels are traps woven from natural materials and employ two cones that fit together so that fish can swim in but cannot leave. By simply tying the funnels together, both facing the same direction, you make the trap easier to open. The same concept will work with a 2-liter bottle; cut off the top and and turn it to the inside to trap smaller bait fish. This type of net is woven like a basket, and the outer piece has a hole in the bottom from which fish can swim into the larger cone where they will get trapped.

LINES WITH L7 TRIGGERS

L7 triggers are simple reverse notches that form a quick-release system. Employing L7 triggers in fishing involves using line and a trap together to actually set the hook after the animal runs with the bait. An L7 trigger is combined with a spring-pole device, allowing the line to be hand-cast off the bank with a baited hook. When the fish or turtle runs with the bait it dislodges the L7 trigger, which springs the pole and immediately jerks the line to set or lodge the hook in the throat of the prey.

TYPES OF PRIMITIVE TRAPS

Most primitive traps work like a simple machine. In fact, you will use some of the five machines discussed in Chapter 3 for constructing them. Understanding your tools will allow you to improvise varieties of traps that adapt to conditions and available game. Deadfall traps will always involve a lever and fulcrum. These bear the weight of the deadfall device and are released by a trigger that many times doubles as a bait stick.

Primitive traps are designed to accomplish at least one of three things: strangle, mangle, or dangle. Many of them use the common releases or triggering systems.

LEANING DEADFALLS

To set a leaning deadfall trap, position a heavy object so that one end leans on the ground, with the weight of the leaning object held up by a trigger device. This device releases the weight of the deadfall device.

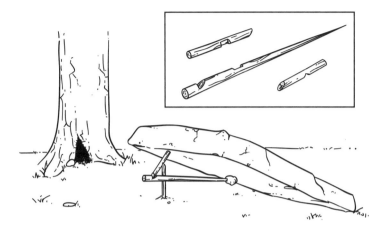

Leaning deadfall

SUSPENDED DEADFALLS

Suspended deadfall traps involve a suspended deadfalling device above the ground that drops upon release. These can be combined with spikes or spear points for larger game.

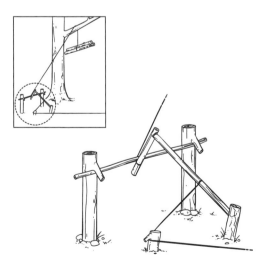

Suspended deadfall trap

Deadfalls are the most misrepresented trap, often poorly illustrated in books and incorrectly taught by instructors. Deadfalling traps are not always intended to instantly kill prey; some of the smaller deadfalls used for microtrapping rodent species will suffocate the animal instead. Confusion over how the animal actually dies is part of the problem. Many people will raise a deadfall like a rock or log at a high angle, thinking this will help them achieve crushing power. The truth is, the higher the angle of the deadfall, the greater the chance the animal will escape the trap before the object makes contact.

There are two simple rules of thumb when employing leaning deadfall devices: The first is that deadfalls should be five times heavier than the weight of the animal to be trapped, and the second is that the deadfall should never be at an angle greater than 30° from the ground. Remember that traps and trap components must match the size of your quarry. When going after a small rodent, don't use a 2″ branch that is too heavy for the animal to pull down or manipulate.

WINDLASS MACHINES (KLEPTSY)

The windlass is used on this trap as a winding device. This creates spring-loaded tension to hold a killing device in place by a bait stick. When the bait stick is removed, it lets the windlass release, swinging the device under tension to kill the target prey.

These traps involve a windlass machine that delivers a killing blow or deploys a spike or spear to impale the animal upon release of the trigger.

FREE-HANGING SNARES

Unpowered snares rely strictly on the animal's struggles to tighten and hold it in the trap. These are often the least effective traps when manufactured in a primitive fashion; however, cable snares in this configuration can be very effective.

POWERED SNARES

Snares involving a spring-loaded engine or a counterweight device can be very effective depending on the setup. They just need to lift the animal off the ground using noncable snares. Remember, an animal will do whatever it can to escape if it is alive, which includes chewing. If the animal is on the ground, it has lots of opportunities to chew its way out of the trap. Most snares will not catch the animal around the neck; more often than not, the snare will encircle the animal's body. Snare loops need to be set at a targeted diameter to ensure a proper catch. A snare set a bit larger than an opossum's head is not likely to catch a coyote. Again, this is why it's important to pay attention to animal sign on the trail so that you know you are setting your traps for the right animals.

TRAP TRIGGERS

Triggers involve the total machine and its operational setup. Following are illustrations of each type of trigger and how to employ the machine into a trap system.

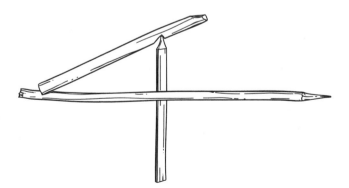

Figure-4 trigger and figure-4 trigger reversed (modified)

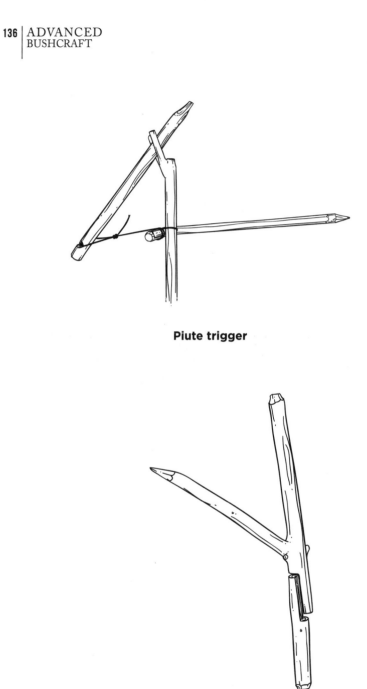

Piute trigger

Split trigger

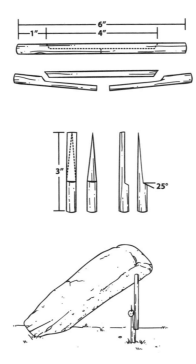

Promontory peg

The L7 trigger is named for the L cut out from the trigger and the 7 cut into the stake. These cuts create a sort of puzzle-piece effect. Each piece is held in place by friction from a spring device that is used to power the trap.

TRAPPING BIRDS

All North American birds are edible and plentiful, which makes them a good choice for your table in a long-term outing. For catching birds, three traps work the best: multiple ground snares, Ojibwa bird traps, and cage-style traps.

MULTIPLE GROUND SNARES

A simple stake in the ground surrounded by a small pile of ground debris can work with a group of small-diameter snares to create a network of ground snares. If you bait them with something on which the birds are feeding, such as small seeds, it is one of the most effective traps for small birds. The biggest challenges to this setup are:

1. They must be small—snares should be made from very fine line.
2. You need a lot of them—at least 25 snares with 2"–3" overlapping loops for a 2' square area.

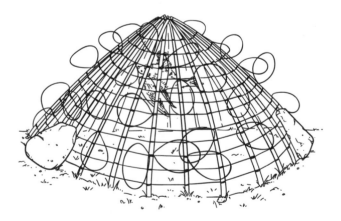

Multiple ground snares

OJIBWA BIRD TRAP

The Ojibwa trap uses a landing perch to lure the bird. The weight of the bird on the perch activates the snare, which in turn traps the bird by its feet. You first need a pole tall enough for a bird to want to land on, but not so tall that you cannot retrieve the bird after it is trapped. Sharpen the pole into a point on both ends. Sharpening will make it easy to drive one end into the ground and will ensure that the bird is not tempted to land on the other end instead of landing on the trigger.

Drill or carve a hole into the top of your pole, about 2" from the point. Place a second stick, about 4" long, into the hole. The diameter of this stick should be just a little bit less than the hole so that the stick rests in the hole rather than being tightly screwed into it. This stick will be the perch. Select a piece of thin cordage about half the length of your pole; this is the snare. It is important that this cord is not too long or else your counterweight will rest on the ground instead of pulling tightly when the snare is activated. Tie a stop knot about one-third of the way into your cord. Use a clove hitch to create a loop in the other side of the knot on your cordage (the longer side). String the cordage through the hole on your pole. Tie a rock that's about the size of the bird you intend to trap on the end opposite of the loop. Place your perch stick into the hole where you have strung the snare. Carefully lay the loop of your snare on the perch. This perch is the trigger stick, and when the bird lands on it the trap will drop the rock and activate the snare. The bird will instinctively grab the stick when it lands, which will ensure that its legs are inside the loop of your activated snare. The big trick to this setup is making sure that the closed snare is drawn close to the upright pole so that when the bird is trapped it is held tight and close in an upside-down position.

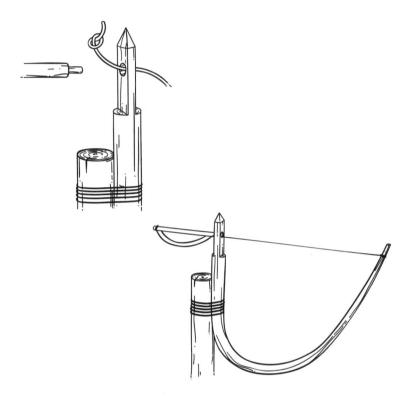

Ojibwa trap

CAGE-STYLE TRAPS

Before building a cage-style trap, you will need to prepare a series of sticks that are similar in diameter but get progressively shorter in length in order to build a cage similar to a pyramid. Make sure the sticks you select are fairly straight and about ½" in diameter. Cut 2 sticks for each of the following lengths: 12", 11", 10", 9", 8", 7", 6", and 5". Finally, cut 6 sticks about 4" long.

Take the 12" sticks and place them parallel to each other, about a foot apart. Attach a length of cord between the two sticks about 1" from their top ends. Attach a length of cord, equal to the first, between the 2 sticks about 1" from their bottom ends. Flip one of the sticks over so that the cords cross each other to form an X.

Push the 11" sticks under the cord, perpendicular to the 12" sticks, until they feel tight against the cord. The four sticks should now form a square. Now push the 10" sticks under the cord and over the 12" sticks until they feel tight. Push the 9" sticks under the cord and over the 11" sticks until they feel tight. Continue adding sticks under the cord, alternating sides like a log cabin until you get to the 4" sticks. Line these sticks in a row next to each other to create a secure roof on your cage. Double-check that there are no gaps on the roof too large through which a bird might escape. If you do see gaps, just fill them in with more 4" sticks.

> **BUSHCRAFT TIP**
>
> One of the main concepts to keep in mind for long-term wilderness living is that live food never spoils. Native peoples of the Americas realized this and began to cage and breed wild turkey and other animals a long time ago. The important thing to remember is that you should not process the food straight away, only care for it while you have it alive. This can be of big advantage in hot weather, but it can also be troublesome if you are in an area with many large predatory animals. This principle is very advantageous when you've caught animals such as turtles and frogs, which can be kept for a time in a sack or bag.

Small tripping lines work well when connected to a step or break-away trigger so that birds set off the trap as they are attempting to hop or duck the strings in order to access the seed bait in the center of the trap. In the right conditions, this type of trap can catch up to ten birds an hour.

HUNTING

Hunting has been used since the beginning of time to secure meat to feed families. It is an art form that in recent times has been spoiled by technology. These days we put too much emphasis on the fastest-shooting bow and the longest-range rifles with expensive optics. It's hard to imagine that not even 200 years ago Native Americans were still hunting buffalo by riding in fields on horseback and shooting them with arrows! Evolving and adapting to our environment is at the core of survival, so there are many benefits to the improvements in hunting practices. Even so, we have also lost many valuable skills such as stalking, closing distance, and tracking prey. These skills demonstrate true self-reliance. In Africa there are tribes to this day that run and track large game animals until the beasts drop from exhaustion and are dispatched by spear. To many of us this would seem inhumane and unnecessary, but to our ancestors it was part of life. True hunting—spotting and stalking on the ground with primitive or improvised weapons—is by far the most difficult way to secure meat, but it can also guarantee food consistently while on the move.

LARGE GAME VERSUS SMALL GAME

The question of whether to hunt large game such as deer or small game like rabbit depends on the situation. Logistically, large game takes large amounts of time and energy both to process and to preserve. Small game can be prepared easily and eaten on the spot if necessary. Large game is a much better option for long-term situations that involve a base camp with an operation for proper preserving.

The other issue that must be considered is the dangers involved in hunting any large game. For example, you're much less likely to be injured by a wounded squirrel than by a wounded hog! Large game, even deer, can be dangerous if you must dispatch them up close. Another consideration is the sheer numbers of available animals. For each deer in a given area there may be ten rabbits, ten squirrels, and twenty chipmunks. Think about the number of birds you see flying away when you walk through the woods compared to deer or other large game you see fleeing.

THROWING STICKS

Many cultures even to this day use throwing sticks of differing configurations for securing small mammals and birds. The **throwing stick** is one of the easiest improvised weapons to create and use effectively, even if you do not have a lot of practice. The biggest convenience of the throwing stick, or rabbit stick as it is sometimes called, is that it can be carried on your belt so that it is out of the way and your hands are free until the second you need it. The reason that the throwing stick is so effective is that it rotates as you throw it so that even marginal shots can be successful. Think about how much easier it is to hit a squirrel with a shotgun compared to a rifle. It is all about surface area!

Throwing sticks are generally about the length of your arm from wrist to shoulder and about 2" in diameter. They can be somewhat bent or they can be straight. The throwing stick kills by inflicting blunt force trauma, so it should always be made of hardwood.

THROWING STARS

This weapon is a further innovation to the throwing stick. The **throwing star** uses two straight sticks with points on both ends that are notched and lashed together to form an X or cross of sorts. This weapon relies on surface area and rotation and can be quite effective even on medium-sized animals such as raccoons. The main drawback to the throwing star is that it is cumbersome and cannot easily be stored, requiring you to hold it while you walk.

SPEARS AND GIGS

Spears and gigs, easily improvised from natural material, work well as weapons. Spear tips can be made by fire-hardening wood or fashioning stone or pieces of glass into sharp points. Many knives now are designed to be used as spear points for emergencies. Of course, then you are giving up your knife to tie it to the end of a pole, so this is not always the best idea. Commercial versions of gigs are available, but they can be easily fashioned from wood. Gigs work well for fishing and underwater use.

SLINGS

You can use any fabric, such as a bandanna or cordage, to make a sling that will allow you to launch a single stone at your prey. This is a frustrating weapon to master due to the limitations of working with one piece of ammunition at a time. It takes a lot of practice. The biggest advantage of using a sling is the abundance of ammunition because any semiround rock you can find will work.

SLINGSHOTS

The **slingshot**, in my opinion, is one of the most inexpensive and practical survival tools for short-term self-reliance. You can purchase commercial folding slingshots or make one yourself very cheaply, and ammunition is available along any creek bank. Slingshots are not difficult to master and fit easily into your day pack. To keep things light, you can even just carry the bands and improvise the frame with natural materials you find on the trail.

TIPS AND TRICKS

1. Use your throwing stick as a multipurpose tool. If you sharpen and fire one end, it can be used as a digging stick and baton.
2. Don't overlook the fact that animal remains can provide tools needed in an emergency situation.
3. When setting deadfall traps, remember the killing device should be five times heavier than the intended prey.
4. One animal will always provide bait or lure to trap others; never waste the glands and guts of any animal.
5. Most animals are easily attracted to a bait not common to the area. For example, if black- or blue-colored berries are common in one area, bait a bird trap with red berries if you can find them. If hickory is the hardwood in an area you plan to trap squirrels, bait traps with walnuts instead.

— Chapter 8 —

PRESERVING
FOOD SOURCES

*"The more survival skills an individual has that have
been practiced physically and otherwise, the better odds
they have for those skills coming to the forefront during
a stressful emergency."*

—CODY LUNDIN, *98.6 DEGREES:
THE ART OF KEEPING YOUR ASS ALIVE!*

The eastern woodlands provide many sources of food to keep
you in good supply during your stay in the wilderness. As you
consider harvesting these resources, it is important to also think of
what can be preserved. Humans have been preserving food since
time immemorial, from cooking a large quantity of meat in order
to make it last for a few days longer to burying it in snow to keep
it fresh. There are a variety of ways to keep meat and process plant
food sources to extend their use.

FLOURS AND MEALS

These plant-based flours can be used in recipes, eaten alone, or added to another grain-based meal. Although plant-based flours are not technically categorized as preserved food, grinding things like acorns is a way of repurposing your resources and extending their life.

ACORN FLOUR

Acorn flour was a staple food item for many native peoples throughout history and acorns remain a major source of food for forest animals today. Its versatility makes it one of the eastern woodlands' best plant-based food resources. I tend to seek out white oak acorns because they have fewer tannins and taste less bitter. **Tannins** within the acorn can give it a very astringent taste. It is important that acorns are processed correctly so they have a gentler flavor.

To process, you must first remove the shells. Crush the acorns with a rock or an axe. Then place the crushed acorns in a bowl of water; the shells will float and the meat will sink. Toss the shells. You want to process the meat down to the smallest-sized granules possible, so you will leach the meat and remove the tannins. To do this, drop the meat of the acorns in a clean batch of boiling water and let it cook until the water becomes brown. This discoloration is from the tannins. Place the acorn meat in another pot of boiling water and repeat the process. Make sure the water in the second pot is already boiling, because if the acorns come in contact with cold water, the process will undo itself. You will likely need to move the acorn meat to a new pot of boiling water three or four times before the staining stops. When the majority of the tannins have been removed, the water will remain clean. If you don't have the necessary tools or setup, acorn meat can be leached in running creek water by placing it in a cloth sack and leaving it in the creek for a week or so. However, the resulting flavor is not as reliable as what you get with the boiling method.

Once the meat is well soaked and clean you can use a stone to grind it into a meal for hot cereal, use it as a bread ingredient, or dry it out and store it for later use. If you decide to save the acorn flour for later, plan to soak it in water before you use it to rehydrate it to its mushy status.

> **BUSHCRAFT TIP**
>
> The tannins that give acorns their astringent taste can be a great resource for other things like medicines and tanning. Save the liquid from the first pot of boiling water you used to leach the acorn meat and reserve it for later use. Astringents work best for external use in a wash or poultice, and the solution will be antiparasitic as well.

CATTAIL FLOUR

Cattail makes the best form of starchy flour that nature has to offer, and the process of extracting it is not overly complicated. First you will need to collect a good bucketful of cattail roots. Loosen the soil around the cattail and its root area. Then put your hand at the base of the stalk and pull to release the entire plant with the root. At this point you can ditch the stalks and just hang on to the roots. Once you have washed and thoroughly peeled them, place them in a bucket of clean water. Here you will begin to break up the roots, which causes the flour to separate from the fibers. Continue until you have separated all the fibers in the roots. As you work, the flour will settle at the bottom of the bucket. Pour out the excess water and dump the remaining mush on a flat surface where it can dry in the sun. Once the flour is completely dry, store it in a cool, dry place away from insects.

CATTAIL ACORN BREAD

2 cups acorn flour
2 cups cattail flour
2¼ teaspoons dry yeast
1½ teaspoons salt
⅓ cup maple syrup
½ cup water
1 cup milk
2 tablespoons vegetable oil

Mix all the ingredients into a dough, shape it into patties, and throw it on some hot ash from your coals to make ash cakes. Wait until the ash is hot enough that it turns white. Brown the ash cakes to your liking, about 3–4 minutes on each side.

NUTS

Rich in protein, nuts are some of the easiest plant-based food resources to harvest.

PINE NUTS

All pine nut seeds are edible, so you do not need to worry about identifying different species. Some have larger seeds than others, and even though you can eat them green, the older ones taste better. The trick is to catch them at just the right time before they drop from the cones. Look for cones that are turning brown but have not yet opened. Arrange them around a fire, and the warmth will force them open so that you can collect the seeds. Just be careful of mildew, which is the enemy of any seed. Keeping them dry is the key.

HICKORY NUTS

Hickory nuts are delicious and especially valuable because their shells efficiently lock out moisture and insects, so they keep for a very long time. Most folks do not care to fool with hickory nuts because they can be difficult to open. Often after all that work you will end up with small pieces of shell everywhere and only a tiny bit of meat. Let me share a secret with you. You have to take advantage of the internal structure of the hull itself to break it cleanly. I prefer to use an axe, but any hammering device—even just a stone—will work.

Turn the nut so that it is lying sideways and the sharp, raised edge is on top. (Basically, turn it to the spot where it wobbles and will not stand on its own.) Then strike the seam in a spot about one-third of the way from the base of the stem. If you follow these steps, you should easily pop the nut into three pieces every time with plenty of exposed meat for the picking.

WALNUTS

Walnuts, specifically black walnuts, are totally different from hickory nuts. If possible, collect them before they fall from the tree and then store them until they turn black. If you do collect any from the ground, inspect them very closely for worm holes. Remove the outer skins from the shells when they turn black and use them for dyes and medicines. Once you have the nut shells, you can then break them open and eat the meat inside. Walnuts do not store in the shell as well as hickory nuts. If you decide to save them for future use, dry them before storing. Leave them in the shell and crack it open just before eating.

FRUITS, VEGETABLES, AND HERBS

You can find a few good fruits (raspberries, blackberries, and blueberries) during certain times of the year in the eastern woodlands. The northern regions tend to have larger varieties. Berries are energizing to eat and add vitamins and fiber to your diet.

FORAGING FOR BERRIES

Take extra care to make certain you can identify any berries before eating them. When in doubt, do not eat!

When looking for berries, scan the area from ground level to eye level. Look for low fruit trees and bushes. A lot of species are creepers, so scan the ground very well. Remember that berry plants are biologically constructed to protect themselves from birds. So they are often hiding under greenery or surrounded with thorns. Keep a close eye out for poison ivy too.

FRUIT	WHERE TO LOOK	SEASON
Blueberries	Blueberries grow in bush form. They flourish in acidic soil, so you can sometimes find them in dried-up beaver ponds or near oak trees. They grow particularly well in sunny meadows.	Flowers in spring, berries in summer.
Elderberries	Moist forest soil along trails and around fields.	Bloom June to July, fruits appear in late summer into fall.
Raspberries	Grow in bushes, usually found in areas that receive full sun.	Blossom in spring, fruit in summer.
Blackberries	Grow in small patches of brambly vines. Look in areas near drainage ditches or trails.	Bloom in midsummer, eat in late summer.
Wild cherries	Grow rapidly from seeds dropped by birds so they are usually found as colonies of trees in clearings.	Blossoms in spring, fruits in summer—often hold until fall.
Cranberries	Grow best in acidic soil and bogs.	Ripen in the fall and usually stay on plant through winter.

Strawberries	Grow close to the ground anywhere.	Blossom in spring, fruit in early summer.
Mulberries	Edges of fields, open woods.	Very hardy, can survive in extremely cold temperatures.
Wild grapes	Occur throughout the eastern woodlands in several species.	Very hard and cold-weather resistant.
Autumn olives	This species is invasive and grows in mostly field edges.	It blooms in early fall and becomes better after the first frost, making it a cold-weather plant.

FRUIT LEATHER

Making fruit leather is the best way to preserve fruit for later consumption when you do not have the resources to set up a canning operation. For this simple process you do not need much more than a sky full of sun.

First mash and grind the fruit into a purée. You can easily remove the seeds by picking them out of the mash with your hands. Spread the purée over a flat surface, like a rock or cutting board that is about ⅛" thick. Leave it in the sun to dry for a few hours. You will know the fruit leather is ready by the glossy look the purée will get when it dries. Store it in a cool place where it will be safe from bugs and moisture. Fruit leather will last a couple months at room temperature but longer if it is kept cool. You can eat it as it is, rehydrate it to make drinks, or use it as an additive for recipes such as bread and cereal.

PLANT SOURCES OF STORABLE FOODS

Many plants provide storable food resources like seeds, seasonings, or bulbs. These food items can be processed and dried for later use.

BULBS

Bulbs can be stored in a cool, dry place for a whole season. There are some great plants with edible bulbs, such as wild garlic or onion garlic, in the woodlands. Ramps and leeks also contain edible and delicious bulbs.

ROOTS AND TUBERS

Cattail contains an edible, starchy tuber that can be eaten as well as stored dry. Arrowhead is another water plant with an edible tuber that has high starch content. Burdock contains a large taproot similar to the potato and can be easily stored for later use if kept dry. Dandelion root makes a good drink or coffee substitute. You can even dry it and grind it down for later use in a hot drink. Yellow nut grass is another edible root plant native around areas of water where cattails and arrowhead are found.

> **BUSHCRAFT TIP**
>
> The center of the cattail shoot is a nutrient-dense, edible resource that makes an excellent vegetable you can simmer in soups or sauté as a side dish. Harvest the cattail shoots in dry weather so that the ground is not too muddy. Select large stalks that have not begun to flower, and separate the outer leaves from the core of the stalk. Discard these tough outer layers until you get down to the soft center. This process requires a lot of peeling, and your hands might get pretty sticky, but the product is delicious and rich in vitamins including vitamin C, beta carotene, and potassium.

WILD SPICES/HERBS

Most wild herbs can be air-dried for later use. You can grind these dried spices into flavorings for food and teas. A few of my favorites are mustard seed, garlic mustard, mint, shepherd's purse, and dock seeds.

SAPS

In the early winter months, many trees can be tapped for their sap, but maples and birches are the best sources in the eastern woodlands. This liquid makes a delicious drink straight from the tree on a cold morning. It can be further rendered into syrup by boiling it down to evaporate the water content.

MAPLE SYRUP

Maple syrup is made by further rendering the sap so that it becomes a sweet, sticky liquid. Maple syrup can be used to sweeten any food or drink and keeps very well if stored properly. Once the sap is collected, pour it into a cooking pot until the pot is about three-quarters full. Boil the sap to evaporate all of the water content. This will take several hours of constant boiling. The most difficult thing about making maple syrup is knowing exactly when the water has completely evaporated and the syrup itself has started to boil. If this happens, the liquid will actually burn. Keep an eye on the color. The syrup should gradually turn gold and then darken until it becomes the mahogany shade of maple syrup. Once the syrup is complete you can strain the liquid to get rid of any particles that may have fallen into the concoction during the long boiling process. Pour into glass jars or plastic containers and store in a cool place. It should last in the refrigerator for about six months.

MAPLE SUGAR

Maple syrup can be even further processed into a delicious sweetener called maple sugar. Bring maple syrup to a boil and skim off the air bubbles as they rise. Reduce the heat a little if it starts to boil over the sides of the pot. When the air bubbles stop appearing, remove the liquid from the heat and transfer it to a wooden bowl. Stir for at least 5 minutes to remove any remaining moisture and then let it stand until it turns hard. This hard material can be ground into sugar and stored in a cool place.

MEAT

Preserving meat, no matter which method you choose, is a critical process because meat spoils very quickly, especially if you do not have access to refrigeration. Here are a few ways of preserving meat from your hunting or trapping campaign so that it can be safely consumed later.

SALT DRYING

The process of drying meat involves pulling moisture from the meat at a slow rate so that the outside of the meat does not dry first. If the outside of the meat dries too quickly, moisture might get trapped inside, which will cause the meat to go rancid. Moisture is the enemy in meat preservation because it allows bacteria to grow. With this understanding, two environmental conditions are necessary for properly drying meat:

1. A humidity level of about 30 percent or less
2. A few straight days with an even temperature where there is little fluctuation from day to night

For this reason, winter in the eastern woodlands is not a good time to air-dry meat. Be careful in the spring that the weather is not too humid. Consider also the meat that will be used. Meats containing high concentrations of fat hold moisture, which makes the fat go rancid quickly. Most meat will contain some fat, but you will find more in animals that are killed during the winter. Be selective and trim away the fat before drying. It is easier to see the fat in red-meat animals like raccoon. You will have to look very carefully when distinguishing between fat and meat in lighter animals such as opossum.

If you do not have the means to cool the meat in a refrigerator, you will need to salt it immediately after it has been gutted. All of the fatty tissue must be removed from the muscle meat before getting started. Then slice each piece of meat into long, thin strips that are similar in size so that you can achieve even drying. Prepare a heavy salt solution into which each strip will be dipped before hanging.

Salt Solution for Drying Meat and Fish
1 gallon water
20 ounces salt

Stir the salt into the water until dissolved.

Dip the strips into the salt solution right before hanging. This solution will add flavor to the meat, speed up the drying, and keep insects away. Suspend the meat strips vertically by the thickest end. Attach them to a line with loops of cordage of a small diameter if possible. Dried meat can then be stored in a breathable bag. You can eat it just as it is or rehydrate right before use.

SUN DRYING

Sun drying works best with fish, but the main concepts are the same for meat. Again, evaporating the moisture from the inside layers to the outside is absolutely critical. Remove the heads and guts and then split the fish right at the spine. Now you should have two pieces, side by side with the skin on top of each. From here, cut the fish into several equal chunks. Fish will generally dry more quickly than red meat, but still dip the strips into the salt solution. Dry the fish strips on racks, which you can easily fashion with two tripods and a cross stick.

The amount of time it takes to dry the fish depends largely on the humidity level in the air. When the fish is completely dry it should crack when you bend it. Test the doneness by bending a corner of the fish after it has been drying on the rack for a day. If you do not hear a crack, let it sit on the tripod for another half day before testing again.

JERKY

You can make **jerky** by adding a good salt solution and some spice to the meat, which is then dried over a low-heat fire of about 120°F. Cut the meat into lean, thin strips. Making jerky is different from salt drying because the goal is to dry the meat with an elevated temperature over a period of time. Hunters used this process long ago because it does not necessarily require salt or rubs (although those extras can give it a sensational taste), and it makes storage and transport so easy. They would eat all they could at the kill site and then dry the rest, which substantially reduces the weight of the meat. If done properly, a pound of meat will reduce to about 4 ounces in weight. When finished, the meat should crack when bent but not snap in half. It should be dry and not moist or greasy.

COLD SMOKING

The **cold-smoking** process is similar to making jerky in that you are cutting meat into thin strips, salting, and drying with an elevated temperature. Here, meat is dried at a temperature that is lower than what you use for jerky—about 85°F. You want a fire with lots of smoke to add flavor (and deter bugs). This method takes 12–24 hours in most cases.

COLD HANGING

In the winter, if the temperatures linger around freezing for a few days, meat can safely hang to dry. The cold temperatures ensure that bacteria do not develop. In this process, the meat does not need to be deboned and cut into strips, but the animal must be completely gutted and opened with a cross stick in the breast so that the carcass stays open while it dries.

TIPS AND TRICKS

1. Be sure to ITEMize any fruit before consumption because many berries are poisonous.
2. Salt can be a major concern for the longer term, but some plants contain enough salt that you can actually extract it by boiling them. Hickory is one tree that will provide salt if the roots are cut and boiled. Once the water has completely boiled away there will be a black substance left that will be salt. Animal blood is another resource rich in salt and many other nutrients. Note that when you extract salt from hickory you will actually be rendering mineral salt. That means it takes a lot to make very little.
3. Many fruits and plants also produce natural dyes. Raspberry will make red, goldenrod is deep brown, pokeberries make a purple dye, bloodroot is orange to reddish. Dyes made from berries can be soaked in a hot fixative of salt water, while most plants will require a vinegar for fixing.
4. Inks for writing can also easily be made from the same plants as dyes, and the color of the berry will generally indicate the resulting color. Pokeberries are the closest to India ink color. To make ink, macerate the berries (poisonous) in a pan or container. Add enough water to cover the material, which should equal about 1 cup in total, and

slowly bring to a boil. Remove from heat, add 1 teaspoon salt, and if available 1 teaspoon vinegar, and simmer 15 minutes. Mix well to dilute the ingredients and strain the liquid into a storage container or bottle that can be sealed. Any large feather can be fashioned into a pen.

5. Anything that will ferment will eventually turn to vinegar. If you need vinegar as a fixative for something, a simple punch made from wild berries can be covered until it ferments (turns to alcohol), then leave it in the open air for a couple weeks and it will turn to vinegar.

— Chapter 9 —
HIDE PRESERVATION, TANNING, AND CLOTHING REPAIR

"Whoever coined the saying 'an ounce of prevention is worth a pound of cure' must have been thinking about survival."

—Brian Emdin, *Survival Secrets*

If you are hunting and trapping during your time in the wilderness, you might also consider using animal hides to manufacture additional resources. Here you'll learn the methods for removing, fleshing, and drying hides as well as how preserved hides can be used.

SMALL HIDES

Small hides from animals such as rabbit, muskrat, and fox are easy to manipulate and can be manufactured quickly. They tend to be too thin for most clothing articles but make sturdy small bags, pouches, quivers, and muffs.

CASING

Casing is a process of removing the hide from the carcass that works well for smaller animals. To case an animal, you remove the skin from the one side of the carcass to the other in one continuous piece, almost like a tube.

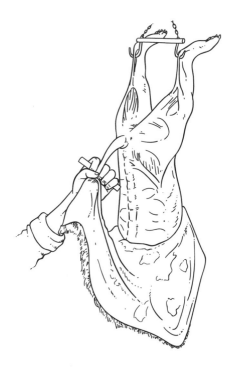

Casing a hide

FLESHING AND DRYING

Fleshing refers to the process of removing all the meat and membrane from the gut side of the hide. Cased hides dry very efficiently on a fleshing beam. **Fleshing beams** can be easily constructed with a large log and a homemade tripod. Find a log about 8" in diameter and strip off all of the bark. Use the tripod to elevate one end of the log. This process is essential because any meat left on the hide will go rancid. If you want to use a hide without hair, to make leather for example, then either pull off the hair during the fleshing process or soak the hide in ash water for a couple of days and then strip the hair.

Once the flesh is removed, you can fashion a small stretcher to dry the hide completely. Stretchers manufactured from wire are available commercially, but they can also be made from flexible saplings.

LARGE HIDES

Large hides from animals such as deer can be split and sewn together for more involved projects like clothing and shelter resources.

SPLITTING

The most effective way to remove a hide from a large carcass is to split the hide. In this process you hang an animal upside down and cut the belly to open the hide with the gut side out. From here you cut across both inside back legs between the anus and vent or penis, and from there you basically strip the hide down off the carcass similar to the way you would pull off a shirt.

> **BUSHCRAFT TIP**
>
> Fleshing knives work well for removing the flesh from a large hide. These knives have a dull, hard edge and are available commercially, or you can use a split bone from the animal itself.

Once all of the flesh is removed, you will need to stretch the large hide on a rack. You can make a square rack from sturdy saplings; it should be at least one-third larger than the hide you plan to stretch on it.

Use your knife to make holes in the edges of the hide, about ½" from the edge so that the hide can dry without tearing. Use any type of cord to lace through the holes and stretch the hide on the stretching rack. Take care to preserve the original shape of the hide as you stretch it.

RAWHIDE

When the hide has been fleshed and dried and the hair has been removed you will have rawhide. Rawhide can be used for many things.

RAWHIDE PRODUCTS

Rawhide is an amazing resource. You can get it wet, form it, and when it dries it will be hard as plastic. It can be used for anything from containers to knife sheaths. Many Native American tribes along the western frontier used rawhide envelopes or bags known as parfleches to carry things such as dried meats, supplies, and clothing. Rawhide can be cut into strips with shears like leather. You can even drive a sharp knife or axe into a tree stump and draw the leather through the blade to split it into two pieces. These strips can be used for lashing projects, twisted into bowstring, or even used for lacing if you slice them narrowly enough.

MAKING LEATHER

From the point of rawhide, you can actually take things a step further into the craft of tanning. You will need to wet the rawhide once more so that it is flexible but not so wet that you have to wring water out of it.

BRAIN TANNING

To tan an animal hide you need tannins, which you can get from the brain of the animal. Heat some water in a pot over the fire but be careful that it does not boil. Cut off a little bit of the brain and mix it into the water very well so that it turns into a paste. Once the paste is ready, you will rub it onto the hide with your hands like a lotion. If you decided to leave hair on the hide, just make sure not to place this paste on the hair side. Once the paste is thoroughly rubbed into the hide, the entire piece needs to be folded up and kept cool for 24–48 hours. The tanning will do its job during this resting period.

After this waiting period it is time to rough the hide. During this process you will squeegee any moisture and material off the hide so that it begins to dry. Spread the hide out on your stretcher or fleshing beam and use a dull hand-scraping device. Once the hide is dry it will need to be stretched and broken by hand. You can tie a rope between two trees and drape the hide over it or hang it over a dull wood stake so that the fibers start to break. When the hide is completely dry and soft you will have garment-grade, brain-tanned leather.

You will need to waterproof the leather or else it will go back to hard-shell if it gets wet. Build a tripod around a small fire that only smolders so that it creates a lot of smoke but not very much heat. Drape the hide over the tripod and fire so that it becomes completely saturated from the smoke and leave it there for a couple of hours. The hide will darken during this time. Take great care not to let the hide get too hot or scorch.

As you can see, making leather is labor-intensive, and keeping many hides in process at different stages makes things go easier. Either way, always be prepared with some manmade fabrics just in case you need something in the short term.

BARK TANNING

Bark tanning is a very complicated process and is not very practical if you are traveling light in the wilderness. I mention it here, however, because a lot of people believe that this is the only true way to produce real leather. This very old tradition was brought over by the colonists from Europe. The most complicated part of bark tanning is the time it takes and the size of the containers needed to accomplish it.

In this process you use tannins from trees such as walnut and white oak to tan the hide. Bark liquor is made by boiling large amounts of bark in three large batches of varying concentrations. The first batch is made very strong and then poured into a 15-gallon storage container. A second batch, a little bit weaker than the first, is poured into another large container. Then a third batch, the weakest yet, is made and poured into a third large container. It takes this much bark liquor for one deer hide.

Soak the hide in the first batch for a couple of weeks. During the first few days you must stir it often and then several times a day after that. The hide is then stored in the second batch of bark liquor for 4 weeks with the same stirring frequency. The hide is stored in the last batch for up to 12 weeks. Winter will be over by the time you get this far. At this point you still need to oil the hide, dry it, break down the fibers, and waterproof. You can see that although bark tanning makes the finest leather, it is a major undertaking.

CLOTHING REPAIR AND REPRODUCTION

When you are out in the wilderness for a long stay there is no question that clothing may need to be repaired. The main purpose of clothing is to provide protection from the elements and environment. Damaged clothing cannot do this job well and will likely only get further damaged over time. In *Bushcraft 101* we discussed the importance of carrying a sail needle and cordage for clothing repairs. For longer-term outings, however, you will require more substantial clothing repair supplies in your kit. You should carry a couple of needles, multiple threads, possibly a small pair of scissors, and a bit of fabric material for patching. You need to think not just about repairs but also construction of new clothing to replace items that cannot be repaired.

Here are the items you should carry:

SMALL CLOTHING REPAIR KIT
- Three different sail needles of varying dimensions
- Several feet of small diameter #6–8 bankline or thread

EXTENDED CLOTHING REPAIR KIT
- Several sail needles in various sizes
- Several glover's needles in various sizes
- Lock stitch awl with spare needles
- Several types of threads from waxed linens to nylon lines
- Scissors
- Shears for cutting thicker materials
- Stitching palm
- Small mallet or maul
- Spiked awl
- Beeswax
- Cloth tape measure
- Several square feet of canvas, wool, and cotton

REPAIR STITCHES

Here are some basic stitches that should be useful for any clothing repair project.

LOCK STITCH

A **lock stitch** can be used to quickly mend holes along seams on heavier fabrics such as leather and canvas. The easiest way to make a lock stitch is with a specialized tool called a lock stitch awl, but it can be done manually also. Whatever the length of the stitch needed, you will require about twice that length of thread. Once the first hole is punched, pull half of the thread to the opposite side of the fabric. With the remaining length of thread, make a loop near the hole through which you've just passed your needle. Now pass the needle along with the thread through the loop and pull tight. Repeat this process, and when finished, all of the lock stitches will be on one side of the fabric. To finish, secure your stitching with a double stitch and then a few stitches in the reverse direction.

RUNNING STITCH

A **running stitch** can also be used to repair seams or hems on thinner fabrics like cotton. A running stitch is a simple in-and-out stitch evenly spaced in a line going through one side and coming back through the other with no locking thread. You can use this stitch to connect materials like sleeves to a shirt.

Whip Stitch

A **whip stitch** is used for seams as well and actually goes around the fabric fold in a spiral pattern, rolling the material as the stitch line progresses to create a welt. This is a good stitch for connecting two separate pieces as well as finishing things like tarp edges and jacket seams. It is suitable for very strong material, even on hide materials, brain-tanned hides, and moccasins.

SADDLE STITCH

A **saddle stitch** is used mainly for heavy materials such as leather. It involves two needles, one on each end of the thread or cord, that pass through the same hole in opposite directions to create a locked running stitch. When using this type of stitch you will want to use a nonawl-type needle and prepunched holes so that the thread passes through the fabric easily without breaking.

SIMPLE CLOTHING PATTERNS

Here are some simple patters that you can use for clothing creation and repair.

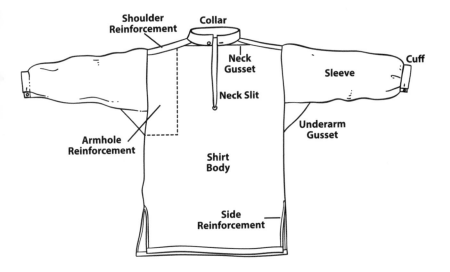

Basic shirt pattern

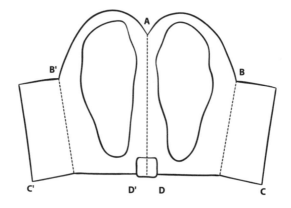

Center seam moccasin

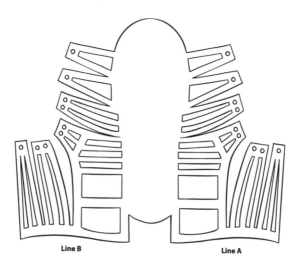

Roman sandal

TIPS AND TRICKS

1. When drying the hair on cased hide it is best to turn the hide hair side out as soon as the raw side is fairly dry but not yet hard.

2. Hair removal will be easier if the hide is soaked in a solution of water and hardwood ashes for a few hours.

3. Shirt patterns can easily be altered to create a larger overgarment such as a blanket shirt. It can then be split down the center with a hood of two triangles added to make a capote.

4. Moccasins will wear quickly so use the thickest leather you have for bottoms and sew an additional sole layer to the outside if possible.

5. Any leather that is left from a project should be cut into lacing so that you always have spare and nothing is wasted.

— Chapter 10 —

WOODWORKING

"Give me six hours to chop down a tree and I will spend the first four sharpening the axe."

—ABRAHAM LINCOLN

Woodworking is one of the most vital skills the woodsman can possess because it allows you to harvest from the largest natural resource in your environment. To our ancestors, the word *woodworking* was actually synonymous with the word *bushcraft*. As long as you have the proper metal tools, skills, and an understanding of different types of wood, you can craft virtually anything needed to sustain yourself over the long term. In the past, an entire family's livelihood could depend on the woodcrafting skills needed to create items like shingles, stakes, besoms, and chairs. Those that weren't used could be traded for foodstuff and groceries.

TOOLS

Following is a description of some of the most important woodworking tools to include in your kit.

FELLING AXE

A felling axe is a little bit larger than the usual model. At minimum, this axe has about a 3-pound head weight and has a 36"-long handle. This is the best tool for harvesting larger pieces of lumber.

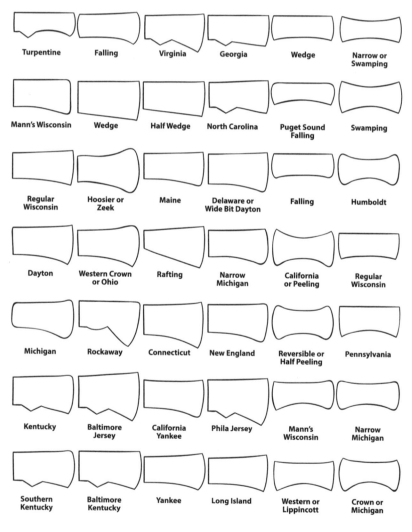

Axe types

BROAD AXE

The broad axe is the best tool for removing the last bit of material from the facing side of a log. It only needs to be sharpened on one side so that it can be used like a chisel. Sizes vary—some broad axes have smaller head weights and short handles, while others are very large. My suggestion is to carry a smaller broad axe and complement it with a larger adze.

ADZE

Adzes are used for flattening the sides of logs and truing the flats. An adze can be used in place of the broad axe in some cases because it works on similar logs but is more versatile. A curved adze can be used for many large-scale carving tasks such as hollowing out large basins or making dugouts.

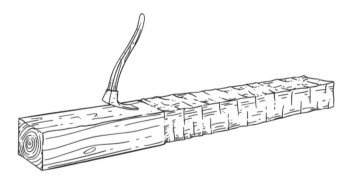

Adze

FROE

A froe is a long, flat blade with an upright handle. This tool is used to split lumber along the grain to create flat pieces of wood such as boards and shingles.

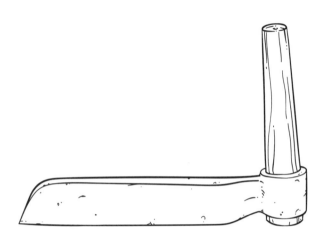

Froe

DRAW KNIFE

The draw knife is very handy when removing bark from a log, and it can also be used to further shape the wood.

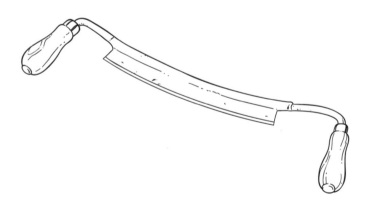

Draw knife

BUCKING SAW

A large bucking or bow saw is used to break down longer logs when creating shingles and smaller lumber boards. The bucking is great for breaking down firewood as well. I recommend the 36" bucking saw.

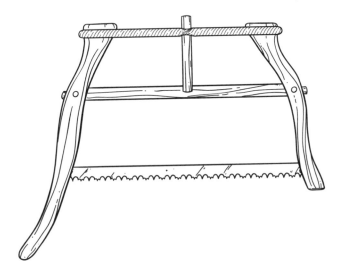

Bucking saw

LOG DOGS

Log dogs are metal-forged U brackets. The sides of the U are right angles, which makes them look square in shape. These log dogs are used to secure a log so that it does not roll while you are working on it. Notch two smaller logs with V cuts and place the working log right in their cutouts. These V cuts will cradle the log. Then pound in the log dogs with a

maul so that one end of the dog is in the working log and one
end is in the cradle log at an angle.

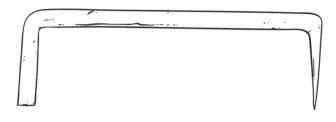

Log dogs

DIMENSIONAL LUMBER

It is often much easier to work with **dimensional lumber**.
Dimensional lumber is wood that has been cut to specific
sizes—for example, 2" × 4"—so that it can be used for building. You can make your own dimensional lumber using simple
wood tools and a large axe.

PROCESSING A TREE TO CREATE LUMBER

Once you have selected a log for your project, lay it on the
ground in your workspace. To make sure the log does not roll,
cradle it in two smaller logs with log dogs attached to each end.
Now you will need to hew the log, or square it. Start by removing
a line of bark from end to end across the face so that you end up
with the thickness that you need. Picture the front of the log as
the top of a stump when you are squaring it. This gives you an
idea of how deep to make that first cut. Clear the bark and pop a
line, using string wiped with charcoal, from end to end. This will
make your cut line clear and visible. Start by making a series of V
cuts with your axe about 2' apart down that cut line on the face

of the log. These V cuts should stretch the entire length of the log. Then remove these 2' pieces with your axe. When the job is completed you should have a rough flat surface on one side of the log. Remove the dogs and turn the log over so that the other side is facing up and reattach the dogs. You can use an adze to square the surface. Repeat this process three more times on the log and you will have one piece of square timber.

Making dimensional lumber

WORKBENCHES

The original workbench was a simple knee-high stump. It seems like a minor amenity, but it provides a flat, stable surface for cutting, chopping, shaping, and anything that can be done with a one-handed tool. The stump vise previously discussed has several advantages and can be used a number of different ways. Many of these are used as bucking logs as well with a V cut channeled out horizontally and a wide kerf cut below the V. A kerf cut is a channel precreated like a jig from a saw cut. It is intended to guide the placement of the next cut. Then smaller materials can be laid within the channel and cut to length. The kerf cut is used as a guide for sawing off material like firewood.

Over time, the construction of these benches has advanced so that they include legs, which makes them more comfortable for sitting but less practical as a place to hang tools and cut wood.

PEASANT BENCH

This simple workbench includes a half-hewn log or flat slab with three or four legs attached. Eventually this evolved into what we now know as the shaving horse. Some peasant benches included a piece of rope that looped around the bench and held the work in place. The worker's foot would hold the loop to the ground.

BESOM

A besom is basically a broom. Old-time besoms were made from a number of different materials. They could be as simple as a whisk-like broom for the hearth or a full-sized floor broom to tidy up around the cabin. Today, European besoms are still made from hazel and small willow shoots. In the eastern woodlands, alder and birch make excellent besom heads. If you have access to an open field, a broom made from long grasses makes an ideal whisk. There are a number of methods for constructing a besom; here's the easiest one:

You will need:

- A 10' length of strong cord
- A good, strong predried sapling of hardwood (like maple) cut to 4'
- Enough head material (such as grasses) to completely fill your hand so that only your thumb and middle finger touch

Align the tops of your head matter and trim the bottom to the desired length. You can even cut this at an angle if you wish to create an angle-headed besom. Once the trimming is complete it is time to wrap the bundle. The best way to do this is to wrap the cord around another stick that you can stand on to pull tension against the bundle as you wrap. Then release a bit of line at a time by lifting foot pressure off the stick. Start with a timber hitch and make several wraps about 4" from the top of the bundle. End this wrap with a clove hitch. Then drop your cordage down about 2" and make another wrap the same as the first. Prepare the handle by sharpening one end to a point. Drive the pointed end of the handle down through the top of the head with a wooden mallet until it passes the second wrap. You now have a besom that should last several months.

AXE AND TOOL HANDLE REPLACEMENT

It is inevitable that tool handles are going to break when you're in a long-term camp. For that reason, you need to understand how to create and replace handles to extend the life of your tools.

Hickory is the preferred wood for straight tool handles. For bent handles, ash is the better wood. For shorter handles or for mauls, maple is a good choice. Handles are generally made from green sapwood. **Heartwood** within the handle may cause warping during the drying and curing process. Some shrinking will occur also, so make handles a little oversized in width. It takes several weeks for green wood to fully dry before the handle can be finally shaped and helved to the tool.

AXE HANDLES

Axe handles are the most common item requiring replacement at any camp. If you can make a good axe handle, all other handle types will be easy for you. Throughout most of history the axe handle was straight, but recently there has been a lot of speculation about the value of the curved dog-leg design and doe- or colt-foot design. Curved handles are helpful for carving-type blades. That said, there is no need to create extra work for yourself unless you want. A straight handle works perfectly with a single-bit axe, but experiment to see what you like in a design and determine what is most comfortable to you. I prefer straight handles for my larger axe and handles with a bit of an arc for my carving axe. All handles have an oval-shaped cross section so that they fit comfortably in the hand. Long handles should be thin so that when they are swung, weight is placed forward. Shorter handles should be thicker to ensure a solid grip.

When making a larger axe handle with a 2½-pound head weight or heavier, start with a hickory log that is about 10" in diameter and 30" long. Split this log and quarter the halves. Then select the best ⅛ section to use for your handle. Next cleave the heartwood from the plank you have selected. If the material is still too thick, cleave it again. The rest of the quarters should be stored off the ground where they can dry out for later use.

For quick short axe handles, you simply need a hewing hatchet and a knife. For longer handles, a drawing knife will give you more flexibility to shape the handle. Start by squaring your wood as best you can, paying attention to the grain lines in order to ensure that the top of the handle has a good straight grain. If you still have the old handle, you can even trace it to make a pencil pattern right on the hickory wood. A shaving horse comes in handy when you are forming the shape of the handle. Don't forget to leave room for the piece to shrink while drying.

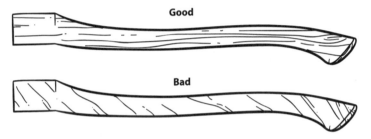

The grain of axe handles should run parallel to the wedge slot.

Axe handle

WEDGE AND HELVING

Before helving the axe you will need to saw a kerf cut from the top of the handle area to insert a wedge after the handle is in place. The wedge should be carved of hardwood and left a little longer than what is needed for it to be even with the handle. On the finished product you ideally want about ¼"–½" of the handle above the eye of the tool. Metal wedges are not essential if the axe is hung correctly and then soaked in hot oil or tallow. Soaking the axe in oil after helving will make the wood swell and also seal it. I recommend that you coat the handle with birch oil after it is completed and hung. Add another coat each week for one month and then coat every month for the first year. This will help maintain the handle and keep it from cracking or drying out over time.

MAKING A WOOD BOW

Before you jump into bow making, please understand that it is complicated. There is a vast difference between a quick bow that lasts a week or two and one that will last until the wood rots. There might be times when you need to manufacture something on the fly, but it is always nice to build a lasting bow. You will learn about both here.

Here are a few terms related to bow construction that you should know:

- **Limbs**—the portion of the bow that bends.
- **Riser**—the static part of the bow that sits in your hand.
- **Belly**—the side of the bow that faces you.
- **Back**—the side of the bow that is farthest away from you when you are shooting.
- **Shelf**—this is a rest for the arrow and can be cut right into the riser or can be added with a piece of bone or wood.
- **String nocks**—the portions at the grooved end of each limb that accept the bowstring and keep it from sliding down the limbs when the bow is strung.
- **Tiller**—the bend of the bow from tip to riser.

The limbs are the portion of the bow that bends, and the riser is static in the hand unless you are building a bow that is purposely meant to bend in the handle area. This works well with green sapling bows for quick use but also adds dramatically to hand shock.

QUICK SAPLING BOWS

Whichever bow you are building, it is critical that construction never compromises the outermost growth ring on the back of the limbs. This ring will give the bow the greatest stability when it is bent on draw and will prevent the wood from splitting. For that reason, choosing the right wood is just as important as proper bow construction. Select a hardwood with a lot of fibers in the grain of the wood, which will add to the durability. Hickory, maple, and red oak are the most common woods used to make a bow. Find a piece of wood that is clear of knots and limbs. Use a sapling that is about 3" in diameter and 6' long. Mark the center of this piece with a knife cut right in the bark. Wrap your hand around the bow with the top of your fist positioned at that mark and then place another mark at the top of your grip.

Now that you have found the center, make sure not to remove any wood from this area. Examine the piece and see if there is already a natural bend in the wood that you can take advantage of. When finished, the profile of your limbs should be almost triangular with rounded corners. Sharp corners are prone to cracking.

When looking at the top and bottom of the riser, you will want the limbs to slowly taper from approximately 3" wide to 1" wide at the string nocks. Use your knife or axe to begin removing material in a slow taper from the riser down to the limb tips. Remember, the more wood you remove, the lighter the bow's draw will be. You want a triangular shape that reduces the length of the limb from riser to the tip. As you go, check the tiller of each limb of the bow. You want the bend to be an even arc. Looking for the curve takes a good deal of practice, and you will probably break a few bows while you are learning. Tiller both limbs so that they bend about 3" in an even arc when you place the instep of your foot on the limb and push on the riser area.

Now it is time to string the bow and begin the final tiller of the bow. Using a string that has ten times the tensile strength of the bow draw you desire is important. For example, if you want a 50-pound bow, you will need a string that has a 500-pound tensile breaking strength. I find that #36 bankline fashioned into two-ply cordage gives about 700 pounds of tensile breaking strength, which is plenty for any bow I would make. When cutting in the string nocks, be careful to make them only as deep as absolutely necessary and angle them at about 45° down toward the riser.

TESTING THE TILLER

To connect the bowstring and string the bow, use a solid loop on one end of the string like a bowline and an adjustable knot like a timer hitch on the other that can be secured with a half hitch. Step through the bow and bring the string up and around the limb tip at the top with the loop already seated in the lower limb nock. Brace the riser area against the back of the knee and bend the limbs equally. Do not try to get the bow to final bracing height. The actual distance of the string from the belly of the riser is usually about 6"–7" at this point. Just string it tight enough for the bow to bend about 3". After this, you can begin to exercise the limbs by slowly drawing the bow with no arrow, a few inches at a time, yet never to fully drawn yet. At this point you are just breaking in the limbs.

The best way I have found to examine the tiller while in the field is to sit on the ground and put the riser of the bow under the instep of your foot. Pull the bow with both hands and look over both limbs as they bend. If the tiller is off and one limb is bending more than the other, you will need to remove small amounts of material from the belly of the stiffer limb. Take care not to overdo it because you will end up with a bow that is too lightweight. After the bow has been stretched about 50–100 times and the tiller appears to be good, you should tighten the string to a brace height of about 5". Start the process of flexing and checking the tiller again. If the bow is too stiff again, remove more material but be careful. If it is good and you complete the exercise process, then you can go to full brace height or 6"–7". The end goal is for the draw to be good enough to hold at full draw until the count of ten. Make sure the tiller is even on both ends.

Remember that at this point you have a green-wood bow and it will take on a permanent bend very easily, so take off the strings when you are not using it. Let the wood dry naturally, and it will eventually mature into a pretty good bow. As it dries it will get stiffer, so eventually you will need to seal it with oil to prevent further drying and possible cracking.

PERMANENT WOOD BOWS

The wood selection process should be the same for a permanent bow. Generally you want to harvest the wood in the spring. Split the log four ways and then you have four possible bow staves. Remove the bark and keep the wood dry and off the ground for at least four seasons. Once the staves are dry, select the best one that does not have any knots or twists. Once the wood is dry, a draw knife, heavy horse hoof rasp, and a shaving horse might come in handy. When working with dry wood, you might actually want to carve a riser and shelf right into the wood. Then carve a flat side into the arrow side of the riser with a small shelf for the arrow—about ½" for the riser and ¼" for the shelf is plenty.

Since the wood is dry, it needs to be treated with great care during this process so that it does not crack. Seal it immediately with animal fat or tallow. Again, never store a wood bow in the strung position; always unstring and lay horizontally across two pegs or forks. Avoid excess heat or direct sun on the bow.

MAKING ARROWS

It is not overly complicated to make arrows. You will need wood, cane, or bamboo between ¼" and ½" thick and about 3" longer than your full draw length. Collect and bundle the shoots with string to help keep them straight while they dry. Once the shoots are dry, remove the bark and check for overall straightness. Heat any crooked areas over the fire and bend them into place with your hand.

Next you will need to choose a hunting tip for the arrow; your selection depends on how you plan to use it. A fishing arrow can be carved into a gig. An arrow for small game can be carved to a fairly blunt point and fire-hardened in the ash and coal below your fire. You will want the largest end of the shaft to be the front. Now it is time to set up the string nock. This will also need to be carved or cut into the arrow. A deep, rounded V will work if you do not have a saw or the ability to carve a nicer notch. Once you have a notch, you can begin to tune the arrows. You might make a lot that do not shoot well. The weight or bend in the shaft might have something to do with this. Select the best ones—the ones that fly about 8–10 yards—and fletch them. Fletching an arrow simply stabilizes the flight path over distance (you do not need to do this process for bow-fishing arrows because they only need to travel a very short distance).

FLETCHING
Fletching is the process of attaching a fletch, usually a feather, to an arrow. You can improvise with duct tape,

but feathers really work best. Collect any feathers you see while you are walking around or harvest them from any fowl you kill for food. Feathers from larger bird species such as turkey and goose work best for this. If you use a standard three-feature fletch, make sure the features come from the same wing because there is a natural bend, called a **helical**, to every feather on the wing. Tail feathers do not have a helical bend, but you should keep those together with their kind too.

You can attach the feather by tying it on with a thin string or using adhesives. It is always a good idea to wrap the area of the arrow that you have notched for placing the string. This ensures that it will not split apart when the arrow is shot. I have found that a leather jig works best for securing the arrow, no matter how it is attached.

Take a 3" square of leather or bark (such as birch) and draw a triangle on it. Find the center point of the triangle and make three slits from the center to the corner of each point. Slide this over the arrow shaft and it will guide you for attaching the feathers. I generally use feathers about 4"–5" long, and they can be cut in any pattern you choose, but wider feathers will slow the arrow's travel more quickly. Large feathers, called flu arrows, are used to keep arrows from traveling long distances in flight when they are being used for aerial or close ground targets. To process the feathers, split down the quill of the feather, which is best done by separating the feather at the top and tearing in opposite directions. This can be done with a knife as well. Once the feather is split, trim it to the desired size and shape it with about ¼" of shaft left bare on both ends.

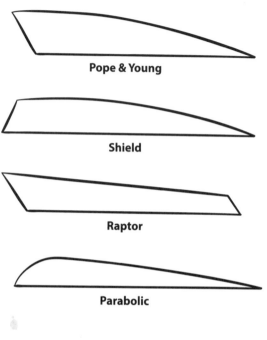

Pope & Young

Shield

Raptor

Parabolic

Fletching

The feathers are then fed through the leather guide and wrapped first at the front toward the arrow tip. They can then be glued or wrapped along the length by moving the guide toward the back of the arrow. Then the butt of the arrow is wrapped with about ½" between the nock and the beginning of the fletching.

STRINGS

As mentioned, the string must be ten times the breaking strength of the bow's fully drawn pull weight, but there are many options for strings: Artificial sinew, bankline, rawhide, and paracord are all options. Just be sure you understand how many strands of each will need to be corded to make a safe bow. To figure this out, you must know the tensile strength of your material.

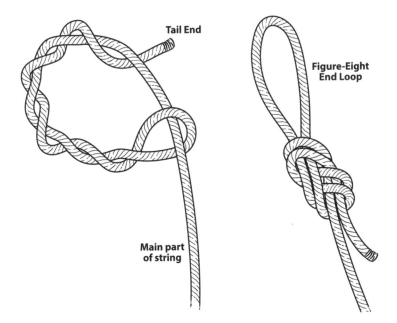

Bowstring and knots

TIPS AND TRICKS

1. If you need a simple pot scrubber, take some broom sedge, fold it in half, and wrap it one time as you would a besom at a point about ½" from the top. Cut it to about 3" total and you will have a great pot and pan cleaner.
2. If you are not sure about the wood density or hardness of the wood you are working, place it in water. Softwoods will float high in the water, while some hardwoods will actually sink.

3. When working with thinner wood or pieces with a smaller diameter, make sure they are fairly dry; otherwise, they will crack over time.

4. Bows should never be left in a vertical position. Always store them horizontally without their strings and with two supports under the limbs.

5. When shooting a bow, mechanics are everything. Be sure to use the same anchor (the location where the draw stops). Like a finger touching a tooth, this will greatly improve consistency.

— Chapter 11 —
BLACK-SMITHING

"I went to the woods because I wished to live deliberately, to front only the essential facts of life, and see if I could not learn what it had to teach, and not, when I came to die, discover that I had not lived."

—Henry David Thoreau

In the old days, the blacksmith was one of the most important people in every village. He alone could manufacture parts for tools such as axes and chisels as well as weapons like knives and swords. Iron was created by smelting in a blast furnace with extremely high temperatures that could liquefy the metal. The liquid ore would run from the bottom of the furnace. In the beginning, this liquid would be diverted into channels in the sand with finger channels emanating from the main channel so that once cooled it could be broken down into manageable pieces. It was said that this configuration resembled a sow laid on the ground suckling piglets; this is where the term "pig iron" originated. This iron was high in carbon and too hard for forging, but it could be remelted and poured into molds, creating "cast" iron. Wrought iron was produced by melting iron in a special furnace and stirring it to remove impurities and carbons. It was then taken from this furnace in a clumped mass and hammered under steam or water to form large lumps of hand-worked iron that could be forged by hammer and anvil.

With all of these methods, the blacksmith was like an engineer. He needed to make precise tools that would aid every member of society from the farmer to the doctor to the hunter and trapper. The ability to manipulate metal has always been a mainstay of survivability.

Today blacksmithing is an endlessly valuable skill that allows you to both repair and create a wide array of resources in the camp setting. If you are in the position to carry blacksmithing tools on your trip, it will be helpful for you to have a basic knowledge of the craft. Here we will discuss the basics that can be most helpful for long-term excursions but will also be convenient for small, quick projects.

BLACKSMITHING TOOLS

Most of the essential tools for small blacksmithing projects can fit into a 5-gallon bucket. Use a metal bucket so that you can repurpose it for quenching as well. Here is a checklist of the most common and useful blacksmithing tools that I recommend keeping in your bucket:

- Anvil
- Hammer
- Bellows
- Forge and fuel
- Pliers or tongs
- Chisel
- Grinding stone

CHAPTER 11 | 195
BLACKSMITHING

- Sand
- Hardy hole
- Pritchel hole

ANVIL

An **anvil** is a hardened flat piece of steel surface upon which you can hammer and form hot metal. A small piece of railroad track works really well as an anvil and can be fashioned with a horn and hardy hole ahead of time. The **horn** is a conical shape attached to the front of the anvil that can be used for forming rings and circular shapes. The **hardy** can be used as an attachment point for other tools like bending forks. If you are not able to source a piece of railroad track, any large chunk of hard steel will work. Even a section of I-beam or other hard steel such as an engine block will do—something that will serve as a hard, flat surface. I would recommend a small block of steel at least 6" × 6" and 2" thick. There are also stump anvils available that drive into a stump; you can even drive a large metal wedge into a stump and use it as an anvil.

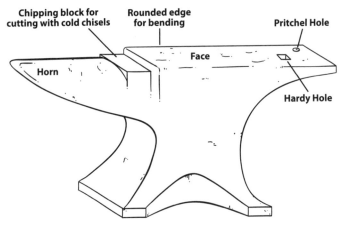

Chipping block for cutting with cold chisels   **Rounded edge for bending**   **Pritchel Hole**

Horn   **Face**

Hardy Hole

Parts of the anvil

HAMMER

A cross-peen hammer, a heavy ball-peen hammer, or a 1½-pound sledge are very useful because they are the most versatile. In extreme cases you could use your axe as a hammer, but you risk damaging the axe or malforming the eye.

BELLOWS

It is best to carry a hand bellows, similar to those used for a fireplace, but you can also improvise this tool. Fanning the forge is what maximizes the heat so that it is possible to bring the metal to forging temperatures. It is possible to fan the fire with a bucket lid or other flat fanning object in a dire emergency, but that will get tiring. If there is a steady breeze, you can build a fire pit in the open and then place a wedge-style tarp at an angle with the back corner set up to force air into the pit like a funnel. Animal skins can be fashioned to create air bags when combined with a tube of bamboo or pipe to force air into a forge as well.

> **BUSHCRAFT TIP**
>
> If you don't have access to coal, you can create charcoal from hardwoods used for forging exactly the same way you make any other charred materials. To do this, you will need a large container as well as a very large and long-burning fire. An alternative is to use normal hardwood in a fire pit and build a large coal bed. If you have forced air, a slit trench–type fire works well here. You can also make a trench above ground with large piles of sand, dirt, or rocks on each side to hold heat better from thermal mass.

PLIERS OR TONGS

You will need something to hold your piece while it is in the forge. A good set of **locking pliers** or a set of heavy **lineman's pliers** will work well for small projects. For larger projects you will need at least one set of **multiple jaw–sized tongs**.

CHISEL

You will need at least one good hot-cutting chisel to cut off metal when heated before you shape it. Other tools along these lines include a couple of punches for drifting eyes in tool heads or punching smaller holes for pinning.

GRINDING STONE

Some sort of rough and fine grinding stones will come in handy for final shaping. These should *not* be the same stones you use for tool maintenance. Natural stones of different grits can be used in an emergency for this process, especially before the metal is hardened.

SAND

Some clean sand will come in handy if you can get the metal to welding temperature, which is white-hot. The sand will be used as a flux for forge welding.

HARDY AND PRITCHEL HOLES

Many anvils have two holes in them: The hardy is square and the pritchel is round. The hardy is used for attaching tools such as cutoffs, bending forks, and cones. The pritchel is for the punch to pass through when punching holes.

SOURCES FOR METAL

You can search around places like old homesteads for scrap melding to be used for your projects. Metals are not all the same, and what you need will depend on the project. As you're searching for materials to repurpose in your blacksmithing efforts, keep an eye out for the following types of metals.

MILD STEEL

Bar stocks and sheet metals are considered mild steels. Nails from fences or old pallets will make good small stock for pins, fishhooks, etc.

MEDIUM-CARBON STEEL

These are harder to locate unless you can locate a junked farm vehicle, but shafting and plow blades are good sources for this type of steel as well as rebar.

HIGH-CARBON STEEL

This is the hardest to come by and, in most cases, the most desirable. It will be your tool steel for making knives, etc. Coil springs, leaf springs, saw blades, old files, Allen wrenches, and any other small tool will most likely be made of high-carbon steel.

The numbers on the chart denote the steel grade and certification system:

RECLAIMED MATERIAL CHART FOR BLACKSMITHING	
APPLICATION	**NUMBER/LETTER**
Agricultural steel	1080
Axels	1040
Ball bearing balls	52100
Ball bearing races	52100
Band-saw blades	L-6
Bits, router	N2
Bolts, anchor	1040
Bolts, heat-treated	2330
Bolts, heavy duty	4815
Brake lever	1030
Cams	A6, S7
Chisels	O2, O6, L6
Clutch disk	1070

Clutch springs	1060
Coil springs, auto	4063
Coil springs, truck	5163
Cold-rolled steel	1070
Connecting rods	1040
Crankshafts	1045
Cutters, bolt	S2, S7
Drifts	L6, S2, S7
Drills	N2
End mills	M2
Fan blades	1020
Files	W-2
Gear shift levers	1030
Hammers	L6
Harrow disk	1080
Hay rake teeth	1095
Jackhammer bits	S5
Knives, machine	M2
Knives, woodworking	O2
Leaf springs	1085, 5160
Lock washer	1060
Mauls	L6, S2
Mower knives	1085
Music wire	1085
Nail sets	L6
Plow beams	1070
Plow disk	1080
Plowshares	1080
Pneumatic tools	L6, A6, S7
Punches, cold	A2, O2
Reamers	M2, O2, A2
Roller bearings	4815
Screwdrivers	L6, S2
Snap rings	1060

Spring clips	1060
Spring steel, clock	1095
Steering arm bolts	3130
Taps	M2, O2
Transmission shafts	4140
Tubing	1040
Universal joints	1145
Valve springs	1060
Wrenches	L6, S2

WORKING WITH HARD METAL

When working with metal, you need to understand how to make it hard and how to make it soft. This process is a bit more complicated than just heating and cooling the material. Metal needs to be heated to a certain temperature/color and then cooled at a certain rate. Many tool steels will also need to be tempered to control how brittle they are so that they can be sharpened.

NORMALIZING

When you begin to work with high-carbon steels, especially when you're making things such as files, it is best to **normalize** them, or bring out some of the hardness, so that they are not brittle. To do this, heat the metal to working temperature and then let it air-cool before heating and forging again.

ANNEALING

This process softens a hard metal such as high-carbon steel so that it can be worked more easily by hammer or grinding. In this process you will heat the metal until it turns bright orange and then place it in some medium such as the cool ashes from an old fire or warm sand where it can cool naturally. Another method is to build a fire and place the metal to be annealed at the bottom of the fire. Use the fire for cooking and other camp activities, then allow it to cool overnight. Retrieve the metal in the morning when the pit has completely cooled. At this point, when it has cooled, your metal will be as soft as it can be. This process can be especially important if you are making knife blades from high-carbon steel. It is done after forging the initial shape so that stock removal can be easily accomplished to form the final profile and grind. The tool is then heat-treated and tempered.

HEAT-TREATING

Heat-treating metal is necessary to achieve the desired initial hardness of the metal before tempering. When metal is heat-treated it must be be taken to a certain color or tested with a magnet to make sure it has reached a nonmagnetic state. Then it will be quenched in a different material depending on desired hardness.

QUENCHING

For a metal to become as hard as it can truly be it needs to be quenched (dunked) in water or some other liquid when the proper color is achieved and then left to cool. Be careful because sometimes this process will make the metal brittle too. Fire steels are generally quenched in water. Oil is a common quench material for most projects, and motor oil will work fine for this if you can find it.

TEMPERING

Tempering steel is a bit of an art. This process requires you to read the color of the metal. When you temper a metal you soften it from its hardened state either in part or in whole depending on the tool. To temper a piece of metal in a forge fire, place the project in the coals of a fire and watch the color change as the material heats up. For example, if working with a knife blade, you would place the blade in a position with the spine against the coal bed and the blade upward. The color of the spine will turn a bluish color. As this color rises to the blade edge, the edge will become a straw yellow color before turning blue. At this point remove the blade and quench it in oil to stop the heating process. The blade is now tempered.

TEMPERING COLORS	
TOOL	DESIRED COLOR
Wood chisels	Pale straw yellow
Hammers	Straw
Drilling tools	Dark straw
Cold chisels and punches	Purple
Springs	Pale blue

MAKING KNIVES

It is easiest to make knives from an existing blade such as a round saw or wide band-saw blade. The beginning shape can be hot cut after the piece is normalized. A full tang knife that will last a lifetime can be fashioned in fairly short order by minimal stock reduction after annealing. Two holes will need to be punched in the handle while it is hot prior to heat-treating and tempering. These holes will be used to pin the handle in place. The final edge should never go on until the very end of the project. Tools such as saw blades and files are already very hard, and many can simply be snapped off to length by bending or striking them with a hammer on the side of the anvil. Fashioning a rat-tail tang knife from a file is one of the easiest ways of making a viable blade and a good starting project to get used to working the metal, heat-treating, and tempering.

MAKING AN AXE

Making an axe from flat stock is a bit more advanced in skill because it requires forge welding to accomplish it correctly. However, you can use an existing tool head such as a ball-peen hammer or roofing hatchet, and then forge to shape it. You will already have the eye and just need to form the blade to the desired profile. Remember that the major difference between an axe and a tomahawk is the way one is mounted to the handle. The tomahawk will require only a rounded eye into which a stick can fit. An axe will require drifting; this means you will force a hole through hot metal with a punch where the handle is wedged into place and inserted from the bottom.

MAKING A FIRE STEEL

To make a fire steel for flint and steel is an easy process; you must, though, use high-carbon steel. You will need to anneal the material first and sand or grind a good clean edge on the striking surface. You can shape the striker in many ways but a typical C is the most common. Once the form you desire is achieved you want to heat the metal to a glowing yellow (not forging heat). At this point quench only the striking edge in water for several seconds, then submerge the entire tool. When finished it should throw sparks well. If not, you did not get the metal hard enough or it was not high-carbon steel. Files make the best strikers. You can always reheat and try again.

BUSHCRAFT TIP

Forge welding is a true skill and takes time to get it right. In forge welding you are heating metal to almost the melting point and then forcing it together with sudden impact while it is still in this near-liquid state. It is amazing to see, like a sparkler show on the Fourth of July. Before attempting this weld you will need to clean the surfaces to be welded with a wire brush, if possible while they are orange-hot. Then add sand for a flux before the final heat to weld.

Now get the metal almost white-hot. It will appear very bright yellow, and a few sparks should be coming from it. Be careful because if you wait a few seconds too long, you will melt off the work in the forge and all will be lost.

Once the welding heat is attained it is critical to get the piece or pieces to the anvil and strike several times. Don't smash the metal with heavy blows; just pound hard enough to compress it when in this near-liquid state. It may require a few more orange/yellow heats to complete the process, but to be effective, a good weld should happen on the first time.

These are the colors you are looking for in the metal when doing forging tasks to form the materials:

FORGING COLORS	
COLOR	**MATERIAL**
Dull red	Hardening or annealing high-carbon steel
Medium red	Hardening or annealing medium steel, minor bends
Bright red	Annealing mild steel
Orange/yellow	Forging high-carbon steel, hot cutting
Yellow	Forging medium steel
Bright yellow	Forging mild steel
Bright yellow (throwing a few whitish sparks)	Welding

OTHER USEFUL ITEMS FROM THE FORGE

- Nails
- Log dogs
- Froe
- Auger
- Raft dog
- Squirrel cooker
- Fire irons
- Hooks
- Holdfasts
- Adze
- Wood chisels
- Mortise chisels
- Brace

— Chapter 12 —
CONTAINERS AND CONVEYANCES

"Climb the mountains and get their good tidings. Nature's peace will flow into you as sunshine flows into trees. The winds will blow their own freshness into you, and the storms their energy, while cares will drop off like autumn leaves."

—JOHN MUIR, *OUR NATIONAL PARKS*

Maintaining a longer-term camp will require restocking with supplies or maybe even moving locations, and for that you'll need containers and conveyances. Here you'll learn to fashion your own, from simple water containers to firing your own clay pots to building watercraft. I grouped containers and conveyances together in one chapter because they both relate to transportation: one to the transportation of goods and the other to the transportation of food.

WATER CONTAINERS

Water containers should be of such material that you can use them to carry water over a distance and also as cooking vessels at camp. Metal tends to be the best option because it can be placed right into the fire. You can also fold over a simple piece of canvas, sew it, and create a container to carry several gallons of water over a distance. Rawhide can be fashioned into a container by a process called **stone boiling** (see the next section). You can also carve and burn containers out of wood. Throughout history, wooden bowls and trenchers have been used for all kinds of liquids. The kuksa, or Sami, cup was carved or burnt from a burl of a birch tree.

POSSIBLE WATER CONTAINERS FOR CAMP
- Birch bark
- Any bark harvested in the spring
- Wood
- Rawhide
- Stomachs of animals (better for carrying than cooking)

> **BUSHCRAFT TIP**
>
> To make a burn container, start a fire on a flat wood surface. Control the circular burn to drive deeper into the material by alternating between burning and scraping the raw material, burning and scraping again, and shaping it into a container.

STONE BOILING

Stone boiling is a process for disinfecting water or cooking food without a metal or nonflammable container. To stone boil you will need to heat rocks in a fire until they are glowing hot and then transfer them to the container of water in order to bring it to boiling temperature. Avoid using rocks found near water or porous rocks such as limestone. Look for rocks that are about fist size or a bit smaller. You can use much smaller rocks if that is all you can find, but know that they will not work as efficiently. Remember that the stones will displace the water, so the size of the container you use will dictate what you can do here. If there is a chance that the container you are using may burn, lower the rocks into the water and hold them for a few seconds before dropping them.

Stone boiling is a messy process and can be dangerous. You will need a good set of tongs or a Y branch with another stick that you can use to manipulate the rocks. Guide the rocks with the plain stick into the Y branch so you can hold them. You need a clean boil, so take care to knock any ash off the rock once it is lifted from the fire before placing it into the container. I have used many different containers, from dry bags to safety helmets, for stone boiling. Almost anything works fine as long as you are careful. Even natural containers will work if you have the time to manufacture them.

You can even use a waterproof tarp to line a hole in the ground and then boil in the pit. Food can be boiled this way too, but it might take a couple of boils for the food to cook properly. Just make sure that the stones are dry and clean from any mud and debris. Get a large fire going with a good bed of coals. Place the rocks on the coal bed and build more fire on top. When the stones glow red, they are ready for use.

BASKETS

Baskets are a fantastic choice for carrying any materials that are not liquid. For thousands of years people used large pack baskets to carry their entire camp! The only limitations are the gaps between the weaves and the size of the basket. A small basket can be used for collecting edibles. Baskets can also be used for certain traps.

CLAY VESSELS

Fired clay vessels are another type of container that has been used for thousands of years. The process for making clay pots is very simple, but every step must be followed carefully and completely because the smallest misstep can compromise the vessel's integrity during and after firing.

PROCESSING CLAY

First you will need to collect a quantity of clay. Unless you are in a clay-based soil area, you will need to go hunting for this. Dig in the mud around creek beds and riverbanks to look for a slick and tacky mud layer. Roll this material into a ball to see if it stays together without cracking too much. If so, this material likely has some clay. Clay can appear in different colors from red to gray to white.

Once you have collected what you believe to be the purest clay, place it in a container of some sort. Back at camp, lay out the clay on a tarp and dry it completely in the sun. After it is dry, crush it as fine as possible and then sift through it with your hands or push it through some mesh to remove any impurities such as stones, sticks, or grass. Remember that a single blade of grass left in the clay can destroy a pot during the firing process. The moisture from the grass will evaporate during the firing and blow a hole in the side of your pot!

To turn this crushed clay into something that can be molded, you will need water and a binder. The binder is what adds some rigidity to the clay and makes it formable. Dry cattail fluff, crushed shell, and sand make excellent binders.

Mix the clay, water, and binder together a handful at a time on a flat surface or a stump. About one-third of the mix should be binder; add just enough water to make the clay easy to mold so that it does not crack during the pot-making process. You have reached the correct consistency when you can roll out a pinky-sized coil and tie it in a loose knot in an over-and-under fashion without cracking it. Wet your hands with a little bit of water to smooth out rough areas of the pot. Make sure there are only rounded corners and never sharp angles. Once the pot is formed it should be left in the sun or set close to a fire until it dries thoroughly.

> **BUSHCRAFT TIP**
>
> Coil pots are attractive and easy to make. Start with a flat round of clay similar to a pancake. Roll a long tube out of the rest of the clay and then wrap it around the base as coils, stacking them until you reach the desired height. Smooth the inside of the pot using some water on your fingers. To make a pinch pot, start with a ball of clay that is suitable for the size pot you need to make. Place your thumbs into the center and progressively pinch the clay all around, pinching and pulling the clay between your thumb and fingers. Keep pinching and pulling outward from the center, forming the pot until it reaches the desired size.

FIRING CLAY

Once the pot is dry both inside and out, top and bottom, it is ready to be **fired**. I have found that resinous woods like pine work very well for this process because they fill the pores of the pot very efficiently and create a kind of glaze over the finished product. Start by putting your pot in the center of the area where you plan to build the fire. Try to elevate the pot from the ground with a platform of sticks. Next build a fire around the pot, engulfing it in heat. Be careful that a large log or stick from the fire does not fall on it during the firing. Use lots of smaller sticks because this fire will need to burn for a couple of hours. After that, let the fire extinguish completely, burning down to ashes and cooling before you attempt to disturb or remove the pot. It's very easy to break pots in the process, so my advice is to make several at a time to ensure that at least a couple survive. Do not even think about adding handles at this point! Keep them simple because you will have greater success.

JACKWARE
Leathers can also be fashioned into containers called **jackware**. First draw a simple pattern similar to the bottom of an hourglass with a 2"-long neck and 1" width. Make two holes on either side of the container so that you can add rope handles later. Leave extra room for a double row of stitches all the way around the leather, except at the opening. Use the pattern to cut out the leather; then get it soaking wet so that it can be formed. Sew the container so that only the opening at the top of the neck remains. Then fill the formed and sewed container with sand that has been heated in the fire. Pack it in very tightly with a ramming stick (any stick about 1" in diameter will do). Pack the sand to the very top of the container and allow it to dry for a few days. Once it is dried, pour out the sand and rinse the container quickly just to remove any remaining particles.

Pour melted beeswax down the inside seams of the container to seal it tight. You can even make a stopper out of wood if you want to secure it closed. You can also now add your rope or strap for a handle.

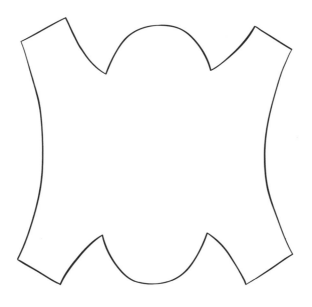

Cup pattern

GOURDS

Gourds cannot be found in the wild, but you can plant them at a permanent shelter or search for them around an older farmstead. Native Americans and pioneers alike used gourds for camp items such as containers, ladles, and cups. Gourds come in many shapes and sizes. Once they are dried, sand or scrape the outer skin from the gourd, cut it open, and scoop out any membranes and seeds. Cut them into any shape you desire and then seal with beeswax.

BOATS

Here are a few different kinds of watercraft that can transport you and your kit if necessary.

RAFTS

A raft is a simple conveyance that can be used to transport you and or your gear over distance in water. Logs work best for this, but since they are round you need to secure at least two together as a stable platform to keep them from rolling in the water. In an emergency, lash (using shear lashings with clover hitches) two or three logs at the end that you plan to straddle while floating down the creek or river. Be very careful about the dangers that lie underneath you as you go—not just animals but snags and rocks that might catch your clothing or legs and pull you from the raft in a current. If you have time to build a more secure raft, lash your logs on both ends. Try to always sit completely out of the water on the raft, even on a hot day. Make sure the raft is wide enough for you to do this. If the amount of cordage you have available is an issue, try using thinner cross members on the ends of the raft and lash those together to lock the logs in place. A third option is to make a catamaran of sorts with a single log in the middle and smaller logs lashed to either side on cross members. Navigate this vessel by pointing the nose of the middle log and using a pole or paddle to guide it down the waterway.

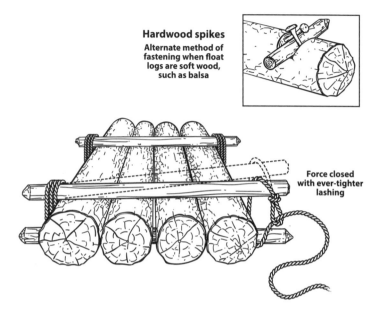

Hardwood spikes
Alternate method of
fastening when float
logs are soft wood,
such as balsa

**Force closed
with ever-tighter
lashing**

Raft construction

DECK RAFT

You can build a deck raft by attaching several logs together to make a larger deck. You can hold this deck together in a variety of ways, depending on the resources you already have on hand. **Log dogs** are metal implements that can be removed when you're done with the raft and taken back to camp for another use. In the old days, these U-shaped brackets would be hammered into two logs that were side by side and then staggered to create a larger raft deck. Nails driven into the cross members on the deck raft make a more permanent setup. You can also lash together the logs and recover the cordage at the end of the trip. Deck-style rafts afford the opportunity to build a steering rudder on the back that is built into a raised bracket. These deck rafts can also be large enough to hold a shelter tent for sleeping. They can also easily be fitted with a seat for long journeys.

SAILING A RAFT

When we talked about building a long-term kit (see Chapter 1), I mentioned the versatility of an **oilcloth tarp**. This material is lightweight enough that it can be used as a sail for your raft. When you are assembling your raft, notch the center log at about 8"–10" into the deck so that a mast can fit into it. Use a green sapling that is about 3" in diameter, and shave the end a little bit so that it screws firmly into this hole. Using the existing tie-outs you have on a Tentsmiths-style tarp, you can lace the tarp up one side to the mast pole. Use a diagonal bracing pole of about 1½" diameter from the mast about two tie-outs from the bottom to the upper corner on the outside of the sail, and then use another piece of rope on the near corner to control the sail into and away from the wind. You can fasten the mast with a loop of rope, but make sure it isn't tied too tight. You want the mast to swing so that the sail can adjust with the wind.

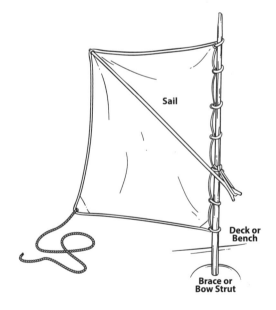

Attaching a sail

RUDDERS

A rudder allows you to steer the boat left or right while traveling. Rudders are essentially long oars that are attached to the back of the raft and sit in the water. You will need a stationary object or bracket to hold the rudder in place for steering. You will also need a fulcrum for the rudder. Both of these can easily be fashioned with a Y branch placed into a hole similar to the mast hole at the rear of the craft.

ANCHORS

Sometimes you may need to anchor your boat if you plan to fish or rest. Making an anchor is incredibly simple, and the materials you choose are at your discretion. A simple bag of rocks on a line attached to the raft will do just fine. You can even improvise something out of railway plates.

PADDLES/OAR

The terms *paddle* and *oar* are often confused, but there is a major difference between the two. Oars generally come in pairs and tend to be longer and thinner and are affixed with an anchoring bracket that can be pinned to a rowing craft. Paddles can be either single- or double-sided and can come in any shape. Paddles are used freehanded to move a craft forward. The type of material from which either paddles or oars are constructed can make a tremendous difference in the ease with which you can maneuver the craft.

BUSHCRAFT TIP

Paddles make it much easier to maneuver a boat, which makes them highly prized watercraft accessories. In fact, handmade Native American paddles were sometimes very ornately decorated and carved works of art. Understanding how to properly carve a wooden paddle is a good skill to own. Hardwoods are preferable for this task.

Use pieces that are at least 6" wide so that they operate as a serviceable paddle. The length is up to you, but start with something that is as long as the distance from your chin to the ground. From there, shorter lengths with wider blades work well as sculling paddles, for example.

BULL BOATS

Some Native American tribes used **bull boats** to move skins, supplies, and firewood from upriver areas back to camp. These boats were lightweight so that they could easily be carried overland and stored until needed. Since the bull boat is round, most navigation is achieved by sculling the paddle. The earliest bull boats were made with a wood frame and covered with a skinned green buffalo hide with the hair on the water side. Once the skin dried into rawhide, it formed a hard outer shell that was waterproof and durable. Many times the tail was left on the hide and used as a tug strap.

These days, making a bull boat can still be accomplished using a tarp or a heavy piece of canvas as a skin. Note that plastic or poly tarps are not a great idea for these crafts because they are likely to tear easily if they get snagged on anything in shallow water.

To build a bull boat, collect several flexible saplings about 1½"–2" in diameter for the frame. First create the hoop size that you want for the finished craft. Eventually this will be the top or the gunnels of the boat. Lay this hoop on the ground and then lash a sapling bent from end to end across the center. Bend four more saplings and lash them at half the distance in both directions. You now have a solid frame that can be "skinned" to create your boat. To add the skin, it is best to turn the frame upright on top of the tarp that you plan to use, drawing all the excess material inside the frame. If you do not have tie-outs on the tarp, use toggles or small stones to secure it tightly inside the frame. To add buoyancy you can make a wreath or flotation circle around the outside of the boat. To construct this wreath, place stakes into the ground and lay bows onto the staked frame, lashing them around the perimeter of the boat. Then finish the frame in the same manner as before and skin it the same way. The advantage to this kind of boat is in the way it floats.

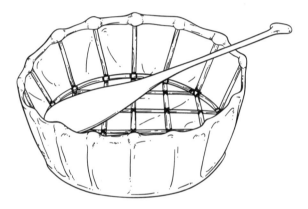

Bull boat

DUGOUTS

Dugouts, essentially canoe-type boats, are among the most resilient of watercrafts. That said, they are also very labor-intensive. You will need a proper tree of lighter wood such as poplar. Poplar wood will be easier to carve or burn out—whichever method you elect to use. Daniel Boone's dugout was made from the yellow or tulip poplar tree. This project requires a good axe and a few other carving tools. Select a log that is at least one-and-a-half times wider than you and about 8'–12' in length. The size really depends on the kind of time you have and the equipment you are carrying.

Once the log is prepared, carve the ends into a wedge shape that will help the vessel cut through water. Then you will remove the bark from the log—a task that is much easier in spring than in winter. Now it is time to hew the log for further processing. Set up a hewing line on the log that is about two-thirds of the way up from the bottom of the log. You can make a simple chalk line by simply rubbing a string with charcoal and popping a cordage down at both sides to create a visible line that will guide you as you cut.

Make a series of V notches down the top of the log about 3' apart and cut down to the line. Turn the log on its side and remove the areas between the V cuts with your axe. This process is called hewing the log and is identical to the process used to make dimensional timber from a round log. Once you have a flat surface, roll the log again to the top and decide what method you will use to make the center cavity where you will sit. Make your decision to burn or carve based on the available tools. If you have an adze tool for digging out the space, use it in conjunction with an axe. Or you can burn down the cavity as you would to make a bowl: burn and scrape, burn and scrape, until you reach the desired depth and width of the cavity. The advantage to digging is that the log will dry more slowly, which makes it less likely to crack.

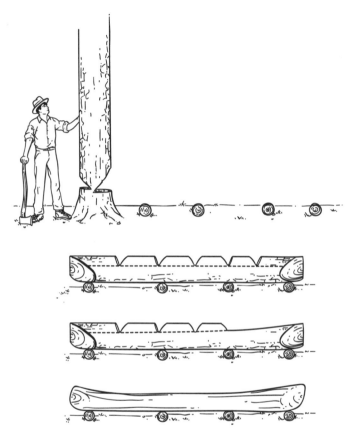

Dugout boat

PACK FRAMES

A pack frame, while not a container or conveyance, allows you to comfortably carry items over distance. Pack frames come in many configurations, from a simple triangle of three sticks to bent-wood hoop frames and pack boards. The ability to remove the pack from the frame and use it for carrying things such as firewood or game is what makes frames invaluable for long-term excursions. You can easily improvise straps for your frame from rope, webbing, or mule tape.

TIPS AND TRICKS

1. When building watercraft, remember that any vessel will need to displace more water by volume than the weight it is intended to carry.
2. Remember, a smaller craft like a bull boat can be made to tow part of your gear if necessary, but *never* put all your eggs in one basket. Carry equipment on a smaller boat that you can tow in case the boat you are riding in tips or flips.
3. Make sure to build your watercraft close to water so that you do not have that far to carry it when it is complete.
4. If burning the cavity for a dugout, cake some mud on the edges near your workspace because this will act as a fire retardant.
5. When conveyance is not possible, you may be surprised at how little weight you can comfortably carry over distance. For the average person, 30 pounds should be your limit. If you can make more than one trip to your camp location with supplies, then each load is lighter and you will be able to bring more equipment.

— Appendix A —
TARP
SETUPS

Following is a quick reference of basic tarp setups to assist you with your camp configuration. This form of temporary shelter, if properly constructed, will keep you safe from wind and precipitation. You can then set up a bed of your choosing to combat ground convection.

Folds	Plan View	Front View	Side View	Back View

2 Pax Hoochi
(low profile storm shelter)

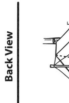

Mini-Tipi

Hammock Basha

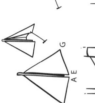

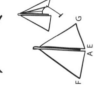

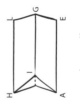

Wedge
(brew shelter)

Paddle/Trek Pole

Reflector
(ideal in woodland with campfire)

Wind

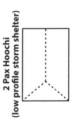

DUTCH-OVEN COOKING

Cast-iron cookware has been a staple of camps since the first North American settlers arrived. The Dutch oven is about the most versatile cooking implement in your long-term kit. In the Dutch oven you can boil, fry, bake, and braise. You can put it right on the fire coals and even flip the lid upside down to use as a skillet for making pancakes!

CARING FOR YOUR DUTCH OVEN

A well-maintained Dutch oven will last you forever. Remember that you should never use soap to clean cast-iron cookery. Clean it gently with running water and wipe out any grease and food bits with a cloth. If it is really well seasoned, you may not even need water to clean it and can just wipe it out after use. Before you even use your Dutch oven, make sure you have seasoned it properly according to the manufacturer's instructions.

SEASONING YOUR DUTCH OVEN

Oftentimes, a Dutch oven will arrive coated in a wax that prevents it from cracking when it is stored and shipped from the manufacturer. To get rid of this wax, place your Dutch oven upside down in a conventional oven that has been heated to 350°F. Do the same with the lid. You might want to put a cookie sheet lined with tin foil under the Dutch oven while you are baking off the wax just in case any residue drops. There tends to be a lot of smoking during this process—do not be alarmed! Once the smoking stops, the Dutch oven is ready to be seasoned. Wash it out with soap and water (this is the only time you will let soap touch it) as soon as it is cool enough to handle.

Seasoning the Dutch oven seals it so that it does not rust and ensures that your food does not take on a metallic taste. Preheat the oven to 425°F. Wipe the Dutch oven down with a rag soaked with some kind of cooking oil such as olive, canola, or vegetable shortening. Make sure you wipe the inside and outside, top and bottom, and do the same for the lid. Bake them in the oven for an hour or so until the smoking has stopped. Repeat this process three times. When you are finished, make sure you give it a once-over to check for any spots that you missed. Every inch of the Dutch oven and its lid should have a glossy finish.

SQUIRREL STEW

6 servings

⅛ pound slab bacon, cubed
1 teaspoon salt
¼ teaspoon pepper
2 tablespoons flour
2 squirrels, cleaned, cut into 6 pieces each
2 large onions, thinly sliced
2 cups beef or chicken stock
Leafy tops of 2 stalks of celery
1 can beans of your choice
2 large ripe tomatoes, peeled
1 cup fresh corn kernels
1 teaspoon Worcestershire sauce

1. Fry bacon in the bottom of your pot until browned, reserving the fat. Set aside.
2. In a medium bowl or on a plate, mix salt and pepper in with the flour. Dredge squirrel in seasoned flour and sauté in the bacon fat until it is brown on all sides.
3. Add onions and cook until soft. Add broth and celery tops. Cover and bake at 350°F for 1 hour.
4. Remove celery tops and add the beans, tomatoes, corn, and Worcestershire sauce. Cover and bake until vegetables are tender—about 30 minutes. Skim off excess fat and thicken gravy with additional flour and ½ cup cold water. Serve hot topped with the bacon.

COWBOY SOUP

6–8 servings

2 tablespoons olive oil
1 pound ground beef
1 medium onion, diced
1 russet potato, diced
1 can peas
1 can green beans
1 can corn
1 can diced tomatoes
1 can baked beans
1 medium onion, diced
Chili powder
Bay leaf
Nutmeg
Salt
Pepper

1. Add the oil to the bottom of your pot. Brown ground beef and onion together. Add remaining ingredients except seasonings. Do not drain vegetables.
2. Put on a low boil until potatoes are fork tender, about 20 minutes. Add seasonings and simmer for another 30 minutes.

POTATOES AND BROTH

6–8 servings

2 cups water
4 cups beef broth
2 pounds new potatoes, peeled and diced

1. Heat water and beef broth to boiling.
2. Place potatoes in the pot and simmer for about 15 minutes or until the potatoes are fork tender. Serve as a soup in the pot.

CORNMEAL BATTER CAKES

About 2 dozen 3" cakes

1 cup yellow cornmeal
½ teaspoon baking soda
½ teaspoon salt
2 large eggs, lightly beaten
1¼ cups buttermilk
2 tablespoons shortening, melted

1. Whisk cornmeal, baking soda, and salt together in a small bowl; set aside.
2. Combine eggs and buttermilk in a separate bowl and then stir into the dry mixture. Stir in melted shortening.
3. For each batter cake, pour about 2 tablespoons batter onto a hot, lightly greased, inverted Dutch-oven lid. Turn when the tops are covered with bubbles and the edges are browned.
4. Serve with syrup, if desired.

FRY BREAD

8 servings

Shortening for frying
2 cups all-purpose flour
½ cup nonfat dry milk
1 tablespoon baking powder
¾ teaspoon salt
¾ cup lukewarm water
Cinnamon
Sugar

1. Melt shortening in Dutch oven for a depth of about 2".
2. Stir flour, dry milk, baking powder, salt, and water together. Knead on floured board. Cover and let stand for 15 minutes.
3. Cut dough into 8 sections, then flatten or roll out to 2" thick.
4. Drop pieces of dough into the hot oil to fry about 2 minutes or until done. Dredge in cinnamon and sugar.

QUICK AND EASY BREAKFAST CASSEROLE

8–10 servings

8 slices bread
2 pounds sausage, browned
16 ounces grated Cheddar cheese
12 large eggs
1 quart milk
1½ teaspoons dry mustard
1 teaspoon salt

1. Line a 12" Dutch oven with tin foil. Lightly grease the foil with butter or oil.
2. Break up the slices of bread into ½" pieces and place them in the Dutch oven.
3. Crumble the cooked sausage meat over bread and cover with cheese.
4. In a separate bowl, mix eggs, milk, dry mustard, and 1 teaspoon salt. Pour the egg mixture over the layered sausage and bread.
5. Cover and bake for 35–40 minutes at 350°F, checking occasionally.

CHICKEN IN A POT

6–8 servings

1 (3–4) pound whole frying chicken
½ teaspoon salt
¼ teaspoon pepper
1 teaspoon poultry seasoning
¼ teaspoon dried basil

1. Wash chicken and pat dry. Sprinkle cavity with salt, pepper, and poultry seasoning. Place in Dutch oven and sprinkle with basil.
2. Cover and bake 4–6 hours at 275°F or until tender.

EASY CHICKEN DINNER ON THE CAMPFIRE

6–8 servings

3 large carrots, peeled and diced
1 head of broccoli, separated into florets, stalks discarded
2 russet potatoes, peeled and diced into ½" pieces
1 whole chicken
1 cup flour
1 tablespoon seasonings of your choice
Oil for frying

1. Cut chicken into 8 parts. Skin chicken.
2. Mix flour and seasonings in plastic bag. Place 2 chicken parts at a time in bag and shake. Remove chicken from bag when coated and repeat until all chicken is coated. Place potatoes in bag and shake. Remove potatoes from bag.
3. Put about ½" of oil in Dutch oven and place on coals. When oil is hot, add chicken and brown on all sides. Pour the rendered fat off the chicken.
4. Add approximately ¼" of warm water. Place potatoes and vegetables over chicken. Cover pot and place back on the coals.
5. Cook for about 1 hour. You will know it is done when the vegetables are tender and the juices run clear when you prick the chicken.

— Appendix C —
CLOUD CHARTS

Reading clouds can help you predict weather systems. Here is a short primer on cloud types.

Altocumulus: These large, gray puffs usually indicate an afternoon thunderstorm is coming. Usually seen in the middle altitude in humid weather.

Altostratus: These gray/bluish clouds cover the entire sky and appear before a weather front in the middle altitude. You really can't see a lot of sun with these clouds—maybe just a little where the clouds are very thin. These clouds usually indicate that widespread, continuous precipitation is coming.

Cirrocumulus: These clouds have a patchy or puffy white appearance. They are ice clouds that appear in the high altitude. They indicate that precipitation is coming within twenty-four hours.

Cirrostratus: These clouds are very thin and look like a halo around the sun or the moon. They are high-altitude clouds full of ice crystals. They indicate rain or snow will arrive in the next twenty-four hours.

Cirrus: These are thin, wispy clouds that appear in the high altitude. They look a little bit like hair. They travel from west to east and indicate that fair weather is coming.

Cumulonimbus: Appearing like giant pieces of cauliflower in the sky, these clouds can produce lightening, thunder, hail, and heavy rain. They can sometimes even form tornadoes.

Cumulus: With their puffy tops and flat bottoms, they indicate fair weather. They appear in the low altitude.

Mammatus: These form under a thunderstorm and look a little like pouches. They are evidence that a storm is weakening.

Stratocumulus: Gray or whitish in color, these clouds have round bases and appear in the low altitude. They hardly ever drop any precipitation.

Stratus: Of all the clouds, these hang the lowest. They are gray and cover the entire sky. They look a bit like fog and sometimes are accompanied by a light drizzle, but they tend not to drop precipitation.

— Appendix D — PRIMITIVE NAVIGATION

W hen in the wilderness, you might find yourself in a situation that requires you to change positions or search out a new area. If you do not have access to a reliable compass, you may need to rely on primitive navigation to find your direction.

There are a few things to remember in navigation:

1. Your shadow can tell you a lot about the direction of the sun.
2. In the Northern Hemisphere, the sun rises in the east and sets in the west.
3. The sun travels a southern arc across the sky, marking the passage of time during the day.

You can put all this together and deduce that when you wake up, the morning sun will be southeast. When you go to bed, the sun will be southwest. During the day, if your back is to the sun, you are facing north. If you are looking at the sun, you are looking in a southerly direction. I say "southerly" because most methods of primitive navigation will point you the correct way but will not give the point of cardinal direction accurately.

RULE OF EQUAL ALTITUDES

To get a correct east-to-west line using shadows, you first need to understand the rule of equal altitudes: *Twice a day— once in the morning and once in the afternoon—the sun will be at the same altitude in its arc across the sky.* Only at these two times will any shadow from a measurement object, like a stick, be the same length. This means that at only two times during the day this measurement object will run perpendicular to a north-to-south line in order to provide a true east-to-west line. You'll need to use any shadow stick for several hours both before and after noon when the sun sets on its southern path.

THE SHADOW STICK METHOD

For ages, the shadow stick method has been the hallmark of primitive navigation. Travelers have used it to first find an east-to-west line and subsequently a north-to-south line. It has been my experience, however, that this method can be highly inaccurate because so many people do not understand the basic rules.

Selecting a Shadow Stick

Select a shadow stick that is at least 2' long. You want something that you can drive into the ground in a flat, unobstructed area so it casts a shadow. Then you can track the shadow's movement while the sun continues on its arc. In the morning, place the stick in the ground and then mark the end of the shadow with a peg or stake. This shadow, in the morning, will be in a westerly direction. Wait at least a couple hours past noon and place another peg in the ground at the end of the shadow. Do this about every hour. After placing the final peg in the ground, lay a stick or a piece of cordage across the two most outside pegs. That is your east-to-west line.

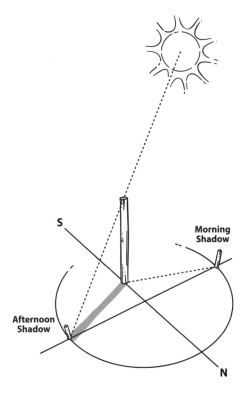

Shadow stick method

TRAVELING SHADOW COMPASS METHOD (PATHFINDER SUN COMPASS)

For a traveling shadow compass, you will select a smaller piece of wood, at least 5" × 7", that will act as a miniature traveling shadow stick. Place this board lengthwise to the east–west line you have made by the shadow stick method.

Drill a hole into the center of the board, and place a small stick in the hole. This stick will cast a shadow on the board. Track the movement of the sun about every hour. As a reference, the sun moves about 15° per hour. This time, mark the end of the shadow right on the board. You can use a round pot or something similar to make the mark almost like you would with a protractor. Then divide these lines into 15° increments starting with the center and then two 45° points for northwest and northeast. Mark everything right on the board. The 90° mark will be on the back of the board. Place a dot on the board every hour through a full day of sun, and then, at the end of the day, connect the dots to form a curved scale. Now you have created your own sundial.

Once all your markings are complete, drill 4 small holes in the corners of the board so that it can be held above ground and kept level. Whenever you need to find a direction or estimate the time, simply hold the board with the back toward the sun and rotate it until the shadow touches the curved line. Set your sundial compass on the ground and this will give you the cardinal directions again from your standing position. Note that this sundial will only be accurate for about 30 days before the shadow length starts to change along with the seasons.

NIGHTTIME NAVIGATION

There are many methods of using the stars and constellations to find direction, but they can all get a little complicated. A good friend of mine, John McCann of Survival Resources, taught me a method called Left, Up, Right, Down (LURD). This allows you to pick any star (except the North Star because it is too high in the sky) and does not rely on any particular star group. Look for a star—not a planet—that is above the horizon but not too high in the sky. As the earth moves, the locations of the stars change, and this movement is the principle behind the LURD method. Find a forked stick that is about 3' in length and a nice, flat place where you can lie down for about 30 minutes. While you lie on the ground, place the stick in the air with the Y facing upwards and use that Y as a viewfinder. Now locate a star in this Y of your stick. Get comfortable and relaxed but make sure you do not move the stick. After about 30 minutes the star will have moved. Here is where the acronym LURD comes in: If the star has moved to the left, you are facing north. If it has moved left and up, you are facing northeast. If it has moved right and down, you are facing southeast. Basically left, up, right, down correspond with the cardinal directions of north, east, south, west.

THE MOON METHOD

You can use the phases of the moon, outside of the new and full moon, to determine direction pretty easily too. Observe any crescent moon and trace a line from tip to tip and then to the horizon. That will give you a southerly direction.

1. Use a string to verify that the two most outside pegs from the shadow stick are an equal distance from the stick for the best accuracy.

2. Solar navigation follows Local Apparent Time, not Standard Time, and may not match your watch if you have one.

3. Your watch can be a direction finder even if it has no hands. If you have a watch, point the hour hand toward the sun and halfway between the hour hand and 12 will be southerly. If you have a digital watch, just draw a watch face with hands on paper to match the one on your wrist.

4. Moss does not always grow on the north side of the tree, but the heaviest vegetation will always point southerly to take advantage of photosynthesis.

5. If you cut down a tree, the growth rings can help with direction finding; the tighter rings will be wider on the southern side.

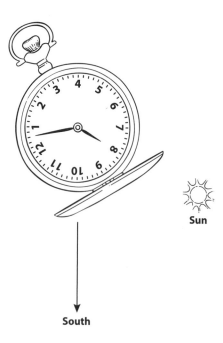

Sun

South

Using your watch as a compass

MAKING A SIMPLE SHADOW BOARD

Deducing general direction from shadows is pretty reliable, but it can be confusing if you have not had a lot of practice. If the sun is sparse or you are on the move, it is often hard to keep track of the shadows. You can make a simple shadow board to help guide you in these situations. All you need is a flat surface, such as a wood plank, with small ridges. Make a circle on the board by tracing a cup or a pot and using an X to divide it into four separate quadrants. Write letters in each of the quadrants in clockwise order: NWSE. This will look a different than a normal compass, but remember that we are dealing with shadow and sun travel. Make a hole in the center of the board and place a stick that will cast a shadow within the circle. Now you can simply hold the board in front of you and turn, directing the shadow to match the quadrant you wish to travel. The front of the board that you have labeled as the northern quadrant will, in turn, be in that general direction. For greater precision, pay attention to the time of day. If the sun is low from morning or evening, you will want to place the shadow more easterly or westerly in the quadrants for greater accuracy.

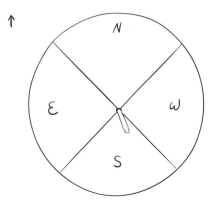

Shadow board quadrants

— Appendix E —

MINERAL

HARDNESS SCALE

MINERAL	MOHS RELATIVE HARDNESS SCALE	SCRATCH TEST	OTHER FACTS
Talc	1	Scrapeable with fingernail	Used in talcum powder
Gypsum	2	Scrapeable with fingernail	Ingredient of plaster
Calcite	3	Scratch with copper coin	Used in cement
Fluorite	4	Scratch with a nail	Used in toothpaste
Apatite	5	Scratch with a nail	Mineral in bone
Feldspar	6	Scratch with steel file	Ingredient in glass, etc.
Quartz	7	Scratches window glass	Used in glass, etc.
Topaz	8	Scratches glass	Gemstone
Corundum	9	Scratches topaz	Rubies and sapphires
Diamond	10	Scratches corundum	"A girl's best friend"

— Appendix F —
MEASUREMENT CONVERSIONS

Here are some simple conversions for the most commonly used units of measure.

CUSTOMARY UNITS	METRIC UNITS
1 inch	2.54 centimeters
1 foot	30.48 centimeters or 0.3048 meter
1 yard	0.914 meter
1 mile	1.609 kilometers
1 ounce	28.35 grams
1 pound	454 grams or 0.454 kilogram
1 fluid ounce	29.574 milliliters
1 quart	0.946 liter
1 gallon	3.785 liters

— INDEX —